MW00527144

The cocktail culture of Italy

APERITIVO

Recipes for drinks and small dishes

MARISA HUFF
Foreword by Joe Bastianich

Photographs by Andrea Fazzari

RIZZOLI
NEW YORK

New York · Paris · London · Milan

To Giorgio and our polpettina

First published in the
United States of America in 2016
by Rizzoli International
Publications, Inc.
300 Park Avenue South
New York, NY 10010
www.rizzoliusa.com

© 2016 Marisa Huff

Photographs © Andrea Fazzari

2020 2021 / 10 9 8 7 6 5 4

Distributed in the U.S. trade by
Random House, New York

Printed in China

Design: Toni Tajima

ISBN-13: 978-0-8478-4744-0

Library of Congress Catalog Control
Number: 2015957042

CONTENTS

FOREWORD

For most Italians, the practice of *aperitivo* is a routine part of everyday life. It's a nod to the end of the day, and like most everything else in Italy, it's done in a thoughtful and regional way.

The Italian art of aperitivo is much more than simply grabbing a drink. It is a fundamental example of Italian sensibility at its finest—an experience that is essentially Italian. It is an encounter, a conversation, slowing down and taking time to savor a drink with friends at the close of the day's labors and enjoying the present moment. Overindulgence is not the point and certainly not the Italian way. In fact, you will never see an Italian drunk during aperitivo. While Italy has certainly contributed to the world's top classic cocktails with the Negroni, Bellini, and the spritz, I am, of course, partial to wine come aperitivo time.

The best aperitivo wines are straightforward, indigenous varietals—simple wines connected to the *terroir* in which they are produced and simply vinified. Personally, I'm more of a white wine guy—especially for a before-dinner pop. Excellent choices include an Arneis from Piemonte, Vermentino from Tuscany, Friulano from Friuli, and Verdicchio from Le Marche. Sparkling is the obvious choice for many to ring in the end of the day, and Prosecco is likely the most widely found, but a great sparkling Ribolla Gialla from Friuli, or an effervescent Erbaluce from Piedmont will also do the trick nicely.

If red is more your fancy, a chilled Lambrusco from Emilia-Romagna or perhaps a Dolcetto d'Alba served at cellar temperature are great options—especially during warmer weather.

On the other hand, aperitivo culture has given rise to a fantastic array of light-style cocktails, and you will find within this book a wonderful selection of recipes for re-creating these at home.

Marisa Huff has brilliantly curated and adapted drinks—as

well as savory small bites—from many of the best aperitivo spots in Italy. I can think of no one better than Marisa to translate the art of the aperitivo for the rest of the world. You can trust that she knows her stuff: I first met Marisa more than a decade ago, when she had a short stint working for Slow Food in Bra, Italy. She was fresh out of school, fluent in Italian, and still wet behind the ears. I hired her to assist with the opening of what was then my newest restaurant in Manhattan, Del Posto. Later she would leave to pursue a career in food writing, beginning with a research position with the esteemed *Vogue* food critic Jeffrey Steingarten. Having worked with some of the best in the culinary industry and perfectly at ease in her adopted home in Padua, which she shares with her Italian husband and their daughter, Marisa is uniquely qualified to serve as your guide to the delights of Italian cocktail culture.

An inspiring combination of recipes and superb instruction, this book expertly conveys to readers why the Italian aperitivo as an experience is so much greater than the sum of its parts.

Joe Bastianich

INTRODUCTION

Ah, Italians: so stylish, so social, and so often late. Everything about them—their love of food, their trim figures, their year-round tans, their fast cars, their questionable politicians, their soccer, their gesticulating, their *aperitivi*—attracts attention and, more often than not, admiration. Although predinner drinking occurs everywhere from Paris to Poughkeepsie, it is in Italy that this social tradition has been raised to an art form.

Picture a flute of bubbly Prosecco topped with fresh white peach puree or a shot of Campari, on the rocks with a twist of lemon. The Italian concept of aperitivo centers on a slightly alcoholic beverage that is intended to whet your appetite for a meal to come. But aperitivo is also just as much about the social act of the cocktail hour itself. As noted author and veteran New York bartender Toby Cecchini describes, "It's a perfect mirror of the country's way with things: simple but dashing."

Simple, dashing, and with a long history. The custom of the aperitivo in Italy can be traced back to the ancient Romans who used to prep their stomachs for lunchtime by drinking wine flavored with honey, a practice they picked up from the Greeks. In more recent centuries, Italian liquorists explored new combinations of herbs, spices, and alcohol, eventually creating enough aromatized wines and bitter liqueurs to fill the Coliseum.

Fortified wine–based aperitifs, such as vermouth, were first developed to mask the flavor of lesser quality wines. Mix subpar wine, a touch of brandy, a little wormwood extract, and about thirty other botanicals and you have yourself a respectable aperitivo. How's that for Italian engineering?

In recent decades, aperitivo has evolved into much more than a predinner drink. It is a daily ritual that draws people together to relax in the company of friends over a glass of wine or a cocktail and something to nibble on.

At cafés (which Italians often refer to as bars), you can expect to find the basics: a Campari and soda or a Venetian spritz. For a glass of wine, an enoteca or restaurant bar is your best bet, while modern mixed drinks should be reserved for cocktail bars. High-end hotel bars are also a safe bet for a well-mixed cocktail, as that is where American and British tourists turned for a stiff drink prior to the arrival of an established cocktail culture in Italy. And during the warmer months of the year, Italians take their aperitivo al fresco, flooding the streets, piazzas, and just about any outdoor space they can find.

Unlike American happy hour, an Italian aperitivo has little to do with dollar tacos and drink specials. It consists of a glass of wine or cocktail and a bite to eat, the goal of which is not to get tipsy or spoil your appetite for dinner. Plus, bars in Italy may actually charge you more, rather than less, for a drink between 6 p.m. and 8 p.m. (9 p.m. during the summer). The markup is justified by the cornucopia of sophisticated Italian bar snacks that accompany your drink in more upscale watering holes (often at no extra charge).

Another thing to consider is that the act of meeting up for an aperitivo is primarily a northern Italian custom. While wine and spirits are produced throughout the country, northern Italians are known to consume more of the stuff. Blame it on what you will—the cooler climate, say, or the influence of Italy's neighbors to the north—but the truth is that you are far more likely to find someone sipping a glass of wine prior to dinner in Piedmont than Puglia. But this doesn't mean you can't order a spritz in Sicily. In recent years, aperitivo has caught on in more cosmopolitan destinations in southern Italy, just the way it has in bars and restaurants in more avant-garde cities across America.

The focus of this book is therefore on the *aperitivi* (the plural of aperitivo) to be had in the northern Italian capitals of Turin, Milan, and Venice. Padua is included, as it is my home and where I have conducted the majority of my research (if enjoying an aperitivo can be called such). I also feature smaller chapter breaks dedicated to Portofino and the Ligurian coast, Florence, and Rome; these provide entry points for first-time visitors who may not make it to the other cities in the north.

So may this book be your guide to a spirited journey across northern Italy, exploring both classic and contemporary Italian cocktails. May it inspire you to dig deeper into Italian culture and encourage you to bring that "simple yet dashing Italian way with things" to your own gatherings at home.

Cin cin!

How to Use This Book

Each chapter focuses on a different city or region filled with recipes inspired by the cocktails and small plates served in specific bars or simple variations on classic regional appetizers or ingredients.

The cocktail recipes all yield one drink, except for those for batch cocktails (pages 204–205), while the food recipes are meant for an aperitivo gathering of about six people. Select two or three food recipes to accompany your cocktail of choice. Feel free to mix and match recipes from various chapters, or decide to focus on your favorite destination (how about a Venetian *cicchetti*-themed party?). When cooking for larger groups, double the food recipes and single out dishes that include instructions for preparing them ahead of time.

Some recipes are simpler than others. If you are new to the kitchen, start with crostini (page 185) or *tramezzini* (page 142), both very Italian and very versatile. Then try slightly more complex recipes like Harry's Bar–style *polpettine* (page 202), focaccia topped with vitello tonnato (page 105), or crispy polenta squares with creamy white fish pâté (page 196). These recipes may take more time, but they will be worth the extra effort.

Start each recipe by prepping your ingredients. All the measuring, washing, and chopping should be done ahead of time, making the cooking experience more pleasurable— especially since your reward for completing a recipe is an aperitivo!

Cocktails should preferably be made fresh so that they don't become diluted due to melting ice. You can either designate a couple of friends to play bartenders for the evening or set up a DIY spritz (page 127), Negroni (page 120) or Bellini (page 171) station. To do so, arrange ingredients and glassware on a counter or tabletop alongside a card with handwritten instructions.

INGREDIENTS

In Italy most recipes begin at the market. When selecting recipes, keep in mind what's in season and what looks most fresh. If you can't find a specific ingredient, feel free to improvise and make substitutions. This holds true for the cocktail recipes as well. It's in the spirit of the Italian cook to use what is available around you. If you don't have Carpano Antica Formula vermouth, try Punt e Mes. If you don't have Parmigiano Reggiano, use Grana Padano, aged pecorino, or another good-quality hard cheese. Also keep in mind that ingredients can vary. If you find your focaccia dough is dry, don't be afraid to add a little water. It may simply be a matter of the protein level of the flour you are using. Recipes in Italy actually call for ingredients based on *quanto basta*, "q.b." for short, meaning, "as much as is necessary," leaving it up to the cook to decide what works.

What you can't find at the market can be purchased from the various vendors listed in the sources section (page 217). A number of staple ingredients like *pane carasau*, pistachios, and jarred olives can be safely stored in your pantry, so stock up for impromptu parties (see also "Shop and Serve," page 95). When possible, buy the best-quality ingredients. What follows is simple advice for distinguishing quality in some Italian staples.

Anchovies

Used in small amounts anchovies can really boost flavor. Their heady, complex flavor adds a dimension of umami and depth of taste to everything they encounter.

Meaty salt-packed anchovies actually taste less salty and fresher than their oil-packed cousins, which were previously salted, then filleted and preserved in oil. Soak salt-packed anchovies in a couple changes of water or rinse well under running water, then carefully remove the fins and bones.

Capers

Capers are the small flower buds of a spiny bush that grows throughout the warmer regions of the Mediterranean. The bud can be preserved in brine, vinegar, or salt. Salt-packed capers are preferable, as they develop more pleasant aromas. Rinse or soak capers in water before using. The fruit of the very same bush, caperberries, are often pickled and eaten on their own like olives.

Frying oil

Many Italian finger foods are shallow-fried or deep-fried. Despite what you may have heard, olive oil can be used for frying. Deep-frying temperatures should be no hotter than 350°F, which is safely below the smoke point of most olive oils.

In the United States this will come at a cost, but it will give your fried foods an authentically Italian taste. But take note that olive oil (even mild) imparts a distinct flavor, which can be a plus in some cases, but some may find it overpowering. Alternatively, you can use other oils with high smoke points, such as cold-pressed neutral oils like grapeseed or sunflower—or a mixture of these with olive oil. Vegetable or soybean oil will also work. After you are done frying, allow the pan to cool and any solids to sink to the bottom. Strain the oil and funnel it back into a bottle. You can use the oil multiple times, as long as it smells fresh and you use it to fry "like" foods. You can also use a mixture of fresh and already used oil.

Olive oil

Good, fresh olive oil is the backbone of Italian cooking. Most of us associate quality with price and the "extra virgin" designation. This isn't entirely wrong, but it certainly isn't enough. "Virgin" means that the oil comes from whole olives that are cold-pressed using machines, rather than chemical solvents or other extraction techniques. "Extra" refers to the grade of the oil and is reserved for oils with an acidity level of 1 percent or less, but that indication doesn't provide any information as to how the oil was handled after production. Olive oil begins to turn rancid quickly with exposure to light, heat, and air, so buy your oil from a reliable retailer who knows and loves the stuff. Ask for help identifying a less expensive, fairly neutral oil for cooking and a more intense oil for finishing or drizzling. Store oil sealed in a cool, dark place. Use within a year of the harvest, which should be clearly labeled on the bottle.

Parmigiano Reggiano

Italians tend to reserve cheese for the end of a meal, Parmigiano Reggiano being the exception. Chunks of real Parmesan from Parma can be identified by the Denominazione di Origine Protetta (DOP) label branded into the outside of the wheel.

Parmigiano Reggiano's flavor changes as it ages, developing more complex aromas. Anything up to twenty-four months is considered young and may smell of fresh-cut grass, while cheese aged over thirty months will be noticeably stronger and saltier. Ask to taste both before you make your purchase from a reliable vendor. Once you get the cheese home, wrap it in plastic and place it in the refrigerator. To serve as part of an aperitivo spread, bring the cheese to room temperature and cut into flakes or chunks using a knife with a short, strong blade.

Salt

All the recipes in this book use fine-grained sea salt. If you prefer to use kosher salt, you will need to double the amount of salt due to its larger, coarser grains.

Flaky sea salt, often labeled *fleur de sel*, is harvested from rock basins that are flooded by seawater. The water evaporates under the sun and salt crystals remain. Although its chemical structure is the same as all other salt, its flaky shape and crunch make it ideal for finishing dishes.

Tuna

Canned tuna is not all created equal. In Italy, blue- and yellow-fin tuna (not albacore) are caught off the coast of Sicily and Calabria. It's cooked and packed in olive oil rather than water, resulting in a silkier texture and meatier flavor. Water tends to leach flavor from fish.

Chapter 1

TURIN

Where it all began

The modern Italian aperitivo can be traced back to the arrival of vermouth in Turin, Italy's first capital located in the northwestern region of Piedmont. In the late eighteenth century, herbal liqueurs were consumed one of two ways: either as a flavoring, in cake or chocolate fillings, or by the spoonful for their medicinal properties, as they were believed to be panaceas for all evils, particularly the wretched unpleasantness of indigestion. We have Antonio Benedetto Carpano, a liquorist or seasoned composer of elixirs and spirits, to thank for inventing an infusion of herbs, roots, barks, and spices inviting enough to make its way from bakeries and pharmacies into the court of the Savoy family and the city's cultured aristocratic salons.

Carpano debuted his proprietary infusion back in 1786 at his small workshop in Piazza Castello, Turin's central square. The fortified wine he called vermouth was just sweet enough and low enough in alcohol to be sipped with pleasure, particularly prior to a meal.

By the mid-nineteenth century, every respectable café, bar, and restaurant in town, including Del Cambio (see page 32), employed its own *maître licoriste*, or master drink maker, who guarded the recipe for the house aperitivo under lock and key.

Today, you can still find vermouth served straight or on the rocks in Turin's historic cafés, but you're equally likely to find it stirred into innovative cocktails prepared by modern mixologists, the *maîtres licoristes* of today.

VERMOUTH

Vermouth is a fortified, aromatized wine—"fortified" meaning that a fairly neutral spirit has been added to raise the alcohol content to between 14.5% and 22% alcohol by volume, and "aromatized" in that the wine has been infused with botanicals. When it comes to vermouth, the principal botanical is wormwood (*Arthemisia absinthium*), often followed by, in no specific order, cinchona bark, rhubarb, gentian, *chinotto*, or myrtle-leafed orange, cola nut, coriander, cardamom, melissa, carnation, pomegranate, elderflower, chamomile, marjoram, ginger, vanilla, hops, and saffron. Like other wine-based aperitifs produced in southern Europe, vermouth was originally made using inferior local wines. The herbs and spices served to improve the flavor.

Italian vermouth was originally made using moscato d'Asti white wine, and still is if you see *Vermouth di Torino* written on the label. The sweetness and signature burnt red color of Italian vermouth, also aptly known as sweet vermouth, comes from the addition of caramel.

Dry vermouth in the French style is also made with a similar neutral white wine but lacks the added sugar or caramel, and is flavored with a different set of botanicals. Although Italy is categorically associated with sweet red vermouth and France with the dry white version, neither country limits itself. The Italian brands Martini & Rossi and Cinzano produce medium-dry Bianco vermouth and a sweet Rosé vermouth in addition to the classic sweet Rosso product.

The origins of vermouth can be traced back to ancient Greece and later Rome, where herb- and flower-infused wines were consumed to calm upset stomachs. Later, with the discovery of distillation, the active ingredients in medicinal plants and the aromatics of all kinds of botanicals, including roots and barks, became easier to extract; alcohol was a better solvent than wine.

To this day, there are those who infuse the wine and then add alcohol, and there are others who extract the botanicals directly into the alcohol, either individually or collectively, then add infused alcohol to the base wine.

Prior to the advent of sweet vermouth, wormwood was prescribed by doctors and herbalists as a "vermifuge," or worm-dispelling agent. The extraction made from wormwood bark was unpleasantly bitter, so diluting it with wine was a major improvement. Antonio Benedetto Carpano's original or "ancient" formula is still being produced by the Fernet-Branca distillery under the label Carpano Antica Formula. Its rich, sophisticated flavor is characterized by notes of vanilla, an ingredient Europeans were particularly fond of in the nineteenth century. Even King Vittorio Amedeo III was known to have had a soft spot for the stuff. It is believed that after receiving a bottle as a gift, he decreed that Carpano's vermouth be brought to the Savoy court, replacing the then popular *rosolio*, an Italian liqueur made from rose petals.

Carpano is also credited with the invention of Punt e Mes, vermouth with an added dose of quinine, a bitter extract made from cinchona bark, more commonly known as the flavoring agent of tonic water.

Twists Taste vermouth neat to identify the citrus flavors already present in the vermouth. Then add a twist of lemon, orange, or grapefruit peel to intensify those aromas or to introduce a new one.

Bitters Bitters can be added to enhance specific aromas in lighter-style vermouths, but are lost on strongly aromatized vermouths like Carpano Antica Formula or Punt e Mes. Look for a standard sweet Italian vermouth, such as Martini & Rossi or Carpano Classico, and begin to play around. Fee Brothers Old Fashion Aromatic Bitters, containing angostura tree bark, is always a good option, as are Angostura bitters, which are heavy on the gentian, and orange bitters. There's a wide range of artisanal bitters available on the market today to experiment with, or you may want to explore the homemade variety. Personally, I prefer to leave it to the professionals who have years, if not generations, of experience in extracting and balancing flavors.

Sweeteners To bring out the inherent sweetness in Italian vermouth, try adding a drop or two of simple syrup or vanilla syrup (see page 51).

Storage Once open, store in the refrigerator. Like any wine, vermouth will begin to oxidize and loose its flavor. It is best consumed within 3 months of opening.

American Cocktails

Visit any watering hole from Alaska to Alabama and you will be sure to find a bottle of sweet Italian vermouth. Its complex yet inviting character is used to balance and blend other stronger liquors.

As cocktail expert David Wondrich describes in his illuminating book *Imbibe*, "Once people noticed vermouth and began poking at it, it was inevitable that sooner or later somebody was going to try to make a Cocktail out of it. After all, this was America, and Cocktails were what we drank."

The first bottles of sweet vermouth arrived in the United States as early as the 1830s, but it wasn't until the end of the century with the arrival of the Manhattan and the Martini that the Italian import secured its spot behind the bar.

The focus of this book, however, is on Italian aperitivo cocktails, both classic and modern, which are lighter than most American libations. The Negroni is the only aperitivo boozy enough to have been invented by a Yankee and one of the reasons it has become a favorite among off-duty American bartenders.

VERMOUTH NEAT

Italian vermouths with more complex flavor profiles, like Carpano Antica Formula or Punt e Mes, are best served this way.

2 ounces sweet vermouth

Serve the vermouth cold from the fridge in a chilled short-stemmed wineglass or cordial glass.

VERMOUTH SPRITZER

Spritzers are seductive little drinks, often leading to a lifelong love affair. As the bubbles tickle the tongue, vermouth's various aromas begin to sing.

1½ ounces sweet vermouth
Soda water
Lemon peel, optional

Fill a rocks glass with 3 or 4 ice cubes. Add the vermouth and top with soda water. Stir and garnish with a lemon twist, if you like.

VERMOUTH ON THE ROCKS

Ice can be both a necessity and a question of personal preference. If you are opening a new bottle of room-temperature vermouth, ice is always a welcome addition. And if you find vermouth to be too syrupy for your taste, ice will help to dilute its consistency and concentration even when served cold from the fridge. In the United States, vermouth on the rocks is commonly served in a narrow tumbler, while in Italy a short-stemmed wineglass is customary.

2 ounces sweet vermouth
Lemon slice or peel, optional

Add an ice cube or two to a narrow tumbler or short-stemmed wineglass and poor the vermouth on top. Garnish as you like.

The people of Turin love their breadsticks, and for good reason. When purchased fresh from the bakery or made directly at home, the long, slender breadsticks Italians call grissini *are light, crisp, fragrant, and absolutely irresistible. Traditionally made with lard for added flakiness, most home cooks choose to use olive oil, but feel free to experiment with both or a combination of the two. Grissini will keep in aluminum foil or in an airtight container for several days. They can also be frozen and recrisped in a 350°F oven for 5 minutes before serving.*

GRISSINI TORINESI

›{ **Makes 6 to 8 aperitivo servings** }‹

1 teaspoon active dry yeast, or
¾ teaspoon instant yeast
(see Note, page 101)

¾ cup lukewarm water

2 tablespoons lard or extra
virgin olive oil

1 teaspoon fine sea salt

2¼ cups all-purpose flour
(or a mix of all-purpose flour and
bread flour in equal proportions),
plus extra for dusting

Using a whisk, dissolve the yeast in the water in a large bowl or in the bowl of a stand mixer. Let stand for 5 to 10 minutes or until small bubbles form. Whisk in the olive oil and salt, then stir in the flour with a wooden spoon.

If kneading by hand, mix until the dough comes together and turn out onto a lightly floured work surface; knead until smooth and elastic, at least 10 minutes, adding more flour as needed to keep the dough from sticking to your hands.

If using a stand mixer, mix on medium speed with the dough hook attachment for about 6 minutes. If the dough sticks to the sides or bottom of the bowl, gradually add more flour until the dough comes together. It should be soft and elastic, but not sticky.

Transfer the dough to a lightly oiled large glass bowl. Cover with plastic wrap and let the dough stand in a warm place until doubled in volume, at least 1 hour. A longer rise time, up to 3 hours, will produce airier breadsticks.

continued —»

Position oven racks in the top rungs of the oven and preheat to 350°F. Lightly oil two large baking sheets. Turn the dough out onto a lightly floured work surface and divide into two equal pieces. Shape each piece into a 4 by 12-inch rectangle, then cut the rectangle lengthwise into twelve 1-inch-wide strips. Gently pick up each strip and pull to the width of a baking sheet. Arrange the ropes 1 inch apart on the baking sheets.

Bake for 20 minutes, then remove the pans and flip the breadsticks so that they will brown evenly. Bake for another 15 minutes or until the breadsticks are golden brown. Let the grissini cool and crisp on wire racks before serving.

Tip If, once cool, your grissini aren't crisp all the way through, return them to the baking sheet and crisp in a 200°F oven for 10 minutes.

Across Italy, bumper crops of summer vegetables are traditionally put up in jars in vinegar-based pickling liquid, sott'aceto, *or in olive oil,* sott'olio. *This quick-pickling recipe is perfect if you want to serve your veggies without the fuss of canning. It can also be made in advance and stored in the fridge for up to three months for impromtu aperitivi. Giardiniera pairs beautifully with a plate of prosciutto crudo or other sliced salumi, but can also be chopped and added to a cold rice or pasta salad.*

QUICK-PICKLE GIARDINIERA

◦{ **Makes about 20 aperitivo servings** }◦

3 cups white wine

3 cups white wine vinegar

2 tablespoons fine sea salt

1 tablespoon sugar

1 teaspoon black peppercorns

2 dried bay leaves

½ head cauliflower, cored and divided into florets (about 2½ cups)

10 cipollini onions, peeled

4 carrots, cut into ½-inch slices (2 cups)

3 stalks celery, cut into 1-inch pieces (1½ cups)

1 yellow bell pepper, stem and seeds removed, cut into 1-inch squares (1 cup)

1 red bell pepper, stem and seeds removed, cut into 1-inch squares (1 cup)

½ cup green beans, cut into 2-inch pieces

In a large pot, bring the white wine and vinegar to a simmer, then stir in the salt, sugar, peppercorns, and bay leaves. Add the cauliflower and onions; cook for 3 minutes. Add the carrots, celery, and bell peppers; cook for 2 minutes. Add the green beans, cook for 2 minutes, then remove from the heat. Cover and let cool to room temperature.

Once cooled, the vegetables are ready to be served, but their flavor improves after soaking overnight in the fridge. To do so, transfer the vegetables and their pickling liquid to a glass container with a lid. To serve, scoop giardiniera into small bowls using a slotted spoon.

The subtle aroma of this saffron-laced cocktail reflects the understated seductiveness of the setting in which it is served. Paneled with dark wood and lit by sconces, Bar Cavour provides a dramatic prelude to a meal at Del Cambio, one of the oldest restaurants in the world.

SAFFRON SPELL

Bar Cavour

1 lime	¾ ounce London dry gin
1 teaspoon natural brown sugar (Demerara or turbinado)	2 ounces cedrata (see page 43) or sparkling lemonade (limonata)
5 mint leaves	Pinch of saffron threads, optional
2 teaspoons saffron simple syrup (recipe follows)	Sprig of mint leaves, optional

Cut the lime into six slices. Place the slices flat on a cutting board and use a paring knife to remove the white membrane in the center of each slice. Muddle the lime slices and sugar directly in a Collins glass. Add the mint leaves and stir with a long bar spoon. Place 4 ice cubes in a zip-top plastic bag and wrap the bag in a kitchen towel. Hammer the ice until it breaks down into pea-size pieces. Fill the glass with the crushed ice, then add the saffron simple syrup, gin, and cedrata. Stir and garnish with a couple of saffron threads and a sprig of mint, or with a garnish of your choice.

Saffron Simple Syrup

⌁{ **Makes 1 cup** }⌁

½ cup sugar	Pinch of saffron powder or 2 pinches of saffron threads

Combine the sugar, saffron, and ½ cup water in a small saucepan. Bring to a simmer over medium heat and stir until the sugar has dissolved. Remove from the heat and let cool to room temperature. Transfer to an airtight container and store in the refrigerator for up to 1 month. Strain before using.

This light, bright summer aperitivo is the fruit of successful international relations. An Italian take on the Caipirinha, the Cocchirinas is made with Cocchi Americano (see below) in place of Brazilian cachaça. If you can't find fresh passion fruit, use a tablespoon of frozen passion fruit puree and reduce the amount of sugar based on the sweetness of the puree.

COCCHIRINHA

Bar Cavour

| ½ lime | 1 passion fruit |
| 2 teaspoons natural brown sugar (Demerara or turbinado) | 3 ounces Cocchi Americano |

Cut the lime half into 3 slices. Place the slices flat on a cutting board and use a paring knife to remove the white membrane in the center of each slice. Place the lime slices and sugar directly in a rocks glass. Cut the passion fruit in half, scoop out the pulp with a spoon, and add the pulp to the glass. Place 3 ice cubes in a zip-top plastic bag and wrap the bag in a kitchen towel. Hammer the ice until it breaks down into pea-size pieces. Add the chopped ice to the glass and top with the Cocchi Americano. Stir and serve.

Cocchi Americano

Americano is an aromatized, fortified wine whose name likely derives from the word *amer*—"bitter"—rather than indicating the American way with things. Think of Americano, the aperitivo wine, as vermouth from another mother. In place of wormwood, the primary botanical is gentian (*Gentiana lutea*), a wild alpine flower. The bitter compounds in gentian root have been proven to stimulate salivation, making them a key ingredient in most Italian aperitivo liqueurs like Campari and Aperol. The bracing bitterness also provides structure to cocktails, balancing out sweetness.

In the United States, Americano is sold under the Cocchi brand. Try serving it over ice with soda water (two parts Americano to one part soda) and an orange peel. The bubbles in the soda water bring out the bitter orange notes.

«— Piazza Vittorio Veneto

Roasted eggplant with crispy blackened edges is a welcome part of any aperitivo buffet. This simple but satisfying recipe can be prepared hours before your guests arrive. The key is to use fresh eggplants that are both glossy and firm. Round globe eggplants can be easily cut into bite-size wedges, but any eggplant variety will do. Use oil sparingly to highlight the natural sweetness of the eggplant.

OVEN-ROASTED EGGPLANT

⊷{ Makes 6 to 8 aperitivo servings }⊶

2½ pounds eggplant
1 teaspoon fine sea salt
Extra virgin olive oil

Trim off the tops of the eggplants and cut the eggplants in half lengthwise. Cut the halves into 1½-inch-thick, 3-inch-long wedges, toss with the salt, and let stand. Preheat the oven to 400°F. Oil a baking sheet or shallow baking pan. Arrange the eggplant wedges flat on the pan and brush the exposed sides with oil. Bake for 25 to 35 minutes, or until the eggplant is soft and the edges have browned nicely. Transfer the eggplant wedges to a serving dish. If the eggplant sticks to the baking sheet, let it cool for a couple of minutes before detaching it with a metal spatula. Serve warm or at room temperature.

*Piedmont has a rich cheese culture that continues to thrive thanks in
no small part to the Slow Food organization, protectors and promoters
of food that is "good, clean, and fair." Every two years, Slow Food
and the small town of Bra, home to the organization's headquarters,
host a four-day cheese festival to celebrate small-production cheeses
from across the region and beyond. Fresh raw-milk goat cheeses or* caprini
*from Valle d'Aosta and Piedmont have a slightly acidic flavor and
can be served covered with olive oil and pepper. Here pink peppercorns
(actually a berry and not a part of the peppercorn family) are added
for color. Serve with a dry white wine, preferably something from
Piedmont like an Arneis or Gavi.*

FRESH GOAT CHEESE AND PINK PEPPERCORNS

✧{ **Makes 6 to 8 aperitivo servings** }✧

**16 to 20 ounces fresh goat cheese
(about 2 logs), at room temperature**

3 tablespoons extra virgin olive oil

**½ teaspoon flaky sea salt,
such as Maldon**

2 teaspoons pink peppercorns

Slice the cheese into 1½-inch-thick rounds and arrange the rounds on a plate. Drizzle with the olive oil and sprinkle with the salt. Lightly crush the peppercorns with a meat pounder and scatter on top of the cheese. Serve with crostini (page 185) or roasted eggplant (page 36).

Bagna cauda (also spelled caoda *and pronounced* BAH-nyah COW-dah) *is something you will rarely find on restaurant menus in Italy. This warm sauce of anchovy, garlic, oil, and butter is generally reserved for the confines of one's home, where a pot can be comfortably placed in the center of the table for the communal dipping of seasonal vegetables, mostly raw but also cooked. Make the sauce the centerpiece of your next aperitivo party and be sure to stock up on bottles of Barbera, traditionally drunk directly from the wine barrel in the fall. Encourage guests to pick up the vegetables and bread directly with their hands.*

BAGNA CAUDA

⊰{ **Makes 6 to 8 aperitivo servings** }⊱

1 cup olive oil

12 cloves garlic, minced

12 anchovy fillets, preferably salt-packed, rinsed

1 tablespoon unsalted butter

Fine sea salt

Crisp, raw vegetables, such as fennel, endive, cauliflower, cardoons, sunchokes, bell peppers, and carrots, for dipping

Crunchy bread, for dipping

Heat the olive oil in a medium saucepan, preferably a terracotta fondue pot, over very low heat. Add the garlic and cook, stirring frequently, for 15 minutes. Finely chop the anchovies, add them to the pan, and simmer for another 15 to 20 minutes, stirring occasionally. Once the anchovies have completely blended into the sauce (if necessary, puree quickly with an immersion or stick blender), stir in the butter to sweeten the sauce. Taste and adjust the salt.

Serve the sauce in the center of the table, ideally over a low flame, or divide the warm bagna cauda between small, individual bowls, refilling the bowls with additional sauce from time to time. Serve the vegetables and bread alongside for dipping.

This "alcoholic merry-go-round" isn't nearly as head spinning as its name might suggest. Created by Italian futurist painter Enrico Prampolini, it is one of a number of futurist cocktails, or polibibite, designed to radically change drinking habits in the early twentieth century with brand-new combinations like red wine, Campari, and cedrata, a citron-infused soft drink (see below). Prampolini would have served his cocktail with a cube of cheese and a cube of chocolate. I prefer a slice of orange, but feel free to experiment, in true futurist sprit.

GIOSTRA D'ALCOL

Caffè Elena

2 ounces dry red wine, preferably Barbera

1 ounce Campari (see page 71)

1 ounce cedrata (see below) or sparkling lemonade (limonata)

Slice of orange, optional

Fill a rocks glass with 3 or 4 ice cubes. Add the wine, Campari, and cedrata. Stir with a bar spoon and finish with a slice of orange, if you like.

Cedrata

>|< Cedrata is a refreshing, slightly sour soft drink flavored with essential oils extracted from the peels of Calabrian citron. In Italy, cedrata is also referred to by the brand name of its most well-known producer, Tassoni. Originally sold as a syrup to be added to sparkling water, Tassoni Cedrata soda holds a special place in the memory of any Italian raised in the seventies and eighties when the soda reached the height of its popularity. In the United States, Eataly carries both Tassoni and an all-natural alternative produced by Baladin, one of Italy's top craft breweries.

Tramezzini, Italian tea sandwiches served without the tea (see pages 142–144), can be found in cafés across Northern Italy. Turin's historic Caffè Mulassano claims to have served the first one back in 1926 after the then owner's wife returned from a trip to the United States, where she likely discovered the wonders of Wonder Bread. To this day, the café's antique glass display case is filled with tramezzini *of all sorts, including the classic Piedmontese pairing of peppers and anchovies (pictured opposite, on left).*

RED PEPPER AND ANCHOVY TRAMEZZINI

Caffè Mulassano

◦{ **Makes 8 tramezzini (half sandwiches)** }◦

4 red bell peppers
2 tablespoons extra virgin olive oil
½ teaspoon fine sea salt
Freshly ground black pepper
8 slices white sandwich bread, crusts removed

4 teaspoons Dijon mustard
24 anchovy fillets, preferably salt-packed, rinsed
4 leaves green-leaf lettuce

Preheat the oven to 375°F. Slice the peppers in half lengthwise, discarding the tops, cores, and seeds. Cut the halved peppers lengthwise into quarters. Transfer to a baking dish and toss with the olive oil, salt, and a couple grindings of black pepper. Bake until soft, about 35 minutes total, tossing after 15 minutes to make sure the peppers are roasted evenly. Let cool to room temperature.

Arrange the slices of bread on a cutting board or other flat surface. Spread ½ teaspoon of the mustard across each slice of bread. Place four pepper slices on one bread slice, arrange six anchovies diagonally across the peppers, top with a lettuce leaf, and close with another slice of bread. Cut in half to make two rectangular tramezzini. Repeat the process to make six more half sandwiches.

If you are planning your first visit to Turin and the surrounding Piedmont region, be sure to go in the fall. Come October, the air has cooled, the fog has settled in, and locally grown tubers, including the prized white Alba truffle, have begun to make their annual appearance. Sunchokes, also tubers, are served sliced raw with bagna cauda (page 40) or enriched with eggs and cream to make decadent flanlike custards called sformati—*from the verb* sformare, *to unmold. To prepare bite-size* sformatini *that can be picked up with one's hands, substitute ricotta for the usual cream or milk and bake the custards directly in the oven, rather than in a bain-marie. If you want to go all out, top with a dollop of fonduta (fondue made with Fontina cheese from neighboring Valle d'Aosta) and sliced white truffle. Sformatini can be prepared in advance and rewarmed in a 200°F oven for 5 minutes. Pair with a glass of Piedmontese red wine, like a young Barbera or Nebbiolo.*

SUNCHOKE SFORMATINI WITH FONDUTA

⊰{ Makes **6** to **8** aperitivo servings }⊱

1 pound sunchokes, peeled and cut into ¼-inch slices

⅓ cup ricotta

3 tablespoons grated Parmigiano Reggiano

1 teaspoon fine sea salt, plus a pinch

Freshly ground black pepper

3 large eggs

Butter, for greasing molds

About 3 tablespoons dried breadcrumbs

½ cup heavy whipping cream

1 cup shredded Fontina d'Aosta (about 3 ounces)

1 egg yolk

Preheat the oven to 325°F. Steam the sunchokes in a steaming basket over a few inches of boiling water for 10 minutes or until tender to a fork. Transfer to a blender or food processor and puree with the ricotta, Parmigiano Reggiano, 1 teaspoon of the salt, and pepper to taste until smooth. Whisk the eggs in a medium bowl, add the sunchoke mixture, and stir to combine.

Grease 24 mini-muffin molds and drop a pinch of breadcrumbs into each mold. Shake to distribute evenly. Divide the *sformato* mixture evenly among the molds and bake for 20 minutes.

Meanwhile, bring the cream to a simmer in a small saucepan. Remove from the heat, add the fontina, egg yolk, and the pinch of salt. Stir until smooth.

When the sformatini are done, let them cool for 5 minutes on a rack. Unmold the sformatini onto a plate. Serve warm with a teaspoon of fonduta on top.

Variations

CELERY ROOT SFORMATINI
Substitute the sunchokes with 1 pound celery root, cutting it into 1-inch squares. Steam for about 15 minutes or until soft, then proceed as described.

ARTICHOKE SFORMATINI
Substitute the sunchokes with 1 (14-ounce) can artichoke hearts drained and rinsed well. Puree the artichokes in a blender or food processor, and taste for saltiness. If salty, do not add more salt. Then proceed as described.

Rabarbaro Zucca is an Italian amaro—a bitter liqueur infused with roots, barks, and flowers intended to be drunk after dinner to aid digestion. The main botanical in this case is rhubarb, followed by bitter orange peel, cardamom, and other mysterious botanicals. Ambrogino, the signature aperitivo at Bar Zucca in downtown Turin, is a nod to Sant'Ambrogio, the patron saint of Milan, where locals have sipped this bittersweet, slightly smoky liqueur since the mid-1800s.

AMBROGINO

Bar Zucca

2 ounces Rabarbaro Zucca

½ ounce Campari (see page 71)

½ ounce vanilla simple syrup (recipe follows)

Splash of soda water

Orange slice, halved, preferably blood orange

Combine the Rabarbaro Zucca, Campari, vanilla simple syrup, and 4 ice cubes in a cocktail shaker. Shake vigorously and then strain into a chilled rocks glass. Top with a splash of soda water, add the orange halves, and serve.

Vanilla Simple Syrup

◦{ **Makes 1 cup** }◦

½ cup sugar | ½ vanilla bean

Combine the sugar and ½ cup water in a small saucepan. Use a small sharp knife to butterfly the vanilla bean; scoop out the seeds with a small spoon. Add the seeds and pod to the sugar water. Bring to a simmer over medium heat and stir until the sugar has dissolved. Remove from the heat and let cool to room temperature. Transfer to an airtight container and store in the refrigerator for up to 1 month. Strain before using.

Note To make basic simple syrup, just omit the vanilla bean and follow the remaining directions.

These petite Italian cheese sandwiches are inspired by the tramezzini served at Bar Zucca. The trifecta of creamy mascarpone, toasted hazelnuts, and white truffles is nearly impossible to resist. Avoid using truffle oil, which is usually made with artificial aromas, and splurge for real white truffle paste, sold in a tube. Pair these tramezzini with a bittersweet Ambrogino cocktail (page 51).

MASCARPONE AND HAZELNUT TRAMEZZINI
Bar Zucca

›{ **Makes 6 tramezzini (half sandwiches)** }‹

1 cup mascarpone (from an 8-ounce/250-gram container)	**6 slices white sandwich bread, crusts removed**
1 teaspoon white truffle paste (see Note)	**½ cup hazelnuts, toasted and chopped**

In a medium bowl, using a fork, mix together the mascarpone and white truffle paste until smooth.

Arrange three slices of bread on a cutting board or other flat surface. Spread the cheese mixture across each slice, dividing it evenly. Close with the remaining bread slices and press down gently so that the cheese reaches the edges of the bread. Cut in half to make six sandwiches. To finish, dip all four sides of each sandwich in the chopped hazelnuts, which will stick to the cheese.

Note To prepare this recipe without using truffle paste, blend ½ cup mascarpone with ½ cup *gorgonzola dolce*, which is creamier and sweeter than regular aged gorgonzola, or *gorgonzola piccante*. The slightly sharp flavor of the gorgonzola makes for a lovely sandwich at a fraction of the cost.

In Piedmont, peppers and anchovies often find their way onto the same plate. The sweet, piquant flavor of peppers pairs beautifully with the rich, briny flavor of the fish. For this preparation, small red peppers or pepperoncini *would traditionally be hollowed out, quick pickled, stuffed, then jarred in olive oil. Pre-pickled Peppadew peppers sold in specialty food shops (or at peppadewusa.com) are a great substitute for fresh* pepperoncini *and save you a considerable amount of time and work. Stuffed peppers can be prepared and stored in an airtight container in the refrigerator for up to 3 days. Let come to room temperature before serving.*

STUFFED PEPPADEW PEPPERS

◦{ Makes 6 to 8 aperitivo servings }◦

1 cup canned tuna in olive oil, not drained (from about three 8-ounce cans)

6 anchovy fillets, preferably salt-packed, rinsed

1 tablespoon salt-packed capers, rinsed and finely chopped

About 2 tablespoons extra virgin olive oil

½ lemon

Freshly ground black pepper

Fine sea salt to taste

24 Peppadew peppers

Drain the tuna, transfer to a medium bowl, and use your fingers to break it apart until fine and uniform in consistency. In a small bowl, mash the anchovies into a paste with the back of a fork. Mix the anchovy paste and chopped capers into the tuna.

Add enough olive oil so that the mixture is moist. Season with a generous squeeze of lemon juice and a couple grindings of pepper. Taste and adjust the salt. Using a teaspoon, fill the peppers with the tuna mixture. Serve at room temperature.

PORTOFINO & THE LIGURIAN COAST

The Saona Libre, an Italian riff on the classic Cuba Libre, is prepared with chinotto rather than Coke. Chinotto is a dark carbonated soft drink made from sour, myrtle-leaved oranges that grow throughout Liguria. The cocktail takes its name from a small island located off the coast of the Dominican Republic called Saona (without a v), which was discovered by Christopher Columbus. The Genovese explorer named the island after the Ligurian seaport of Savona (with a v), hometown of his friend Michele da Cuneo, who would become the island's first governor. Lurisia brand chinotto made with real Savona oranges is sold at Eataly, while San Pellegrino–brand chinotto can be ordered online.

SAONA LIBRE

1 lime, plus 1 wedge for garnish
2 ounces white rum (or dark rum, if preferred)
About 4 ounces chinotto, chilled

Cut the lime into quarters and squeeze the juice of all four quarters into a Collins glass. Add 3 or 4 ice cubes to fill the glass and pour the rum over the ice. Top with the chinotto, garnish with a lime wedge, and stir briefly with a bar spoon.

The Ligurian coast is blessed with fertile soil and sunshine: two ingredients that make for great lemons. So when life gave the owners of Niasca, a small Portofino-based farm, lemons (of the Tigullio variety), they decided to make limonata. *Their sparkling lemonade, which can be found at Eataly, is lightly flavored with elderflower. In the absence of Niasca limonata, try adding a teaspoon of elderflower syrup (see page 131) to other brands of sparkling lemonade to give your Ligurian mojito a floral note.*

LIGURIAN MOJITO

Niasca

½ lemon, cut into quarters, plus 1 lemon slice

½ teaspoon sugar

4 leaves fresh basil

2 ounces white rum

3 ounces Italian sparkling lemonade (limonata), preferably Niasca brand

In a Collins glass, muddle the lemon quarters and sugar. Tear apart the basil leaves by hand and add to the glass. Place 4 ice cubes in a zip-top plastic bag and wrap the bag in a kitchen towel. Hammer the ice until it breaks into pea-size pieces. Fill the glass two-thirds full with the crushed ice and pour in the rum. Top off with the sparkling lemonade and stir. Garnish with the slice of lemon.

«— *Lemon tree at Belmond Hotel Splendido in Portofino*

While Genoa is home to the fluffy white focaccia that most commonly comes to mind when daydreaming of Italy, the most heavenly of all flatbreads can be found about twelve miles south of the Ligurian capital in the small, seaside town of Recco. In bakeries and restaurants throughout Recco and the nearby village of Camogli, home to the Revello bakery, local bakers place soft, tangy cow's-milk cheese between two tissue-paper-thin sheets of dough and bake it in a very hot oven until the dough is golden and the cheese begins to ooze out the cracks. This culinary wonder is known to locals as focaccia col formaggio, *cheese focaccia, or simply* focaccia di Recco, *focaccia from Recco. The key is to stretch the dough until it is transparent without tearing it. This may take some practice. The dough can also be frozen, so consider doubling or tripling the recipe, wrapping additional dough tightly in plastic wrap, and placing it in the freezer for up to three months. The dough can be defrosted overnight in the fridge or for a couple of hours on the kitchen counter.*

LIGURIAN CHEESE FOCACCIA

Revello

•⟨ **Makes 6 to 8 aperitivo servings** ⟩•

⅓ cup extra virgin olive oil, preferably a delicately flavored Ligurian variety, plus extra for greasing and brushing

1¼ cups all-purpose flour

1¼ cups bread flour (see Note)

1 teaspoon fine sea salt

About 1 pound Crescenza or stracchino cheese (or Taleggio or Brie without rind)

Flaky sea salt, such as Maldon, for sprinkling

To make the dough in a stand mixer: Whisk ¾ cup water and the olive oil together in the bowl of the mixer. Add both flours and the salt and, using the dough hook, mix together on low speed until the dough comes together. Continue mixing on low speed for about 10 minutes until the dough is smooth and very elastic.

To make the dough by hand: Whisk ¾ cup water and the olive oil together in a medium bowl. Add both flours and the salt and mix by hand until the dough comes together, then transfer to a flat work surface dusted with flour. Knead the dough for at least 15 minutes until the dough is smooth and very elastic.

Shape the dough into a ball, cover with plastic wrap, and set aside for at least an hour, until it doubles in size.

If you have a pizza stone, place it in the oven, then preheat the oven to 500°F.

Meanwhile, grease a large baking sheet lightly with olive oil. Divide the dough into two equal-size balls. Place one ball on a floured work surface. Use a rolling pin to roll the dough into a rectangle. Once the dough is as thin as possible, lift it up and continue to stretch the dough with your hands, draping it over your knuckles and pulling outward. Toss the dough back and forth a few times in order to stretch it in all directions. If the dough rips, squeeze it back together. Once the dough is paper thin, lay it over the prepared pan.

Arrange rows of tablespoon-size clumps of cheese across the dough, leaving about an inch between each clump. Ideally the cheese will melt to cover the dough completely during baking.

Roll out the remaining ball of dough as you did the first. Place the second sheet of paper-thin dough over the cheese. Using the rolling pin, seal the edges of the dough and then tear or cut off the excess dough from around the edges. Pinch holes into the top layer of the dough for steam to escape during baking.

Brush the top with olive oil and sprinkle with a little flaky sea salt.

Bake for 10 to 12 minutes or until the focaccia is golden with some darker brown spots. The cheese may ooze out of the air holes in the focaccia. You may need to use a wooden spoon or spatula to punch down the dough if it puffs up in areas during cooking.

Remove the sheet pan from the oven and transfer the focaccia to a cutting board by gently sliding it off the pan with the help of a pizza peel. Cut into 3 by 4-inch pieces using a knife or pizza wheel and serve hot. The focaccia should be soft and oozing with cheese.

Note This recipe can be prepared using only all-purpose flour. Note that the dough won't be as strong and is more prone to tearing when stretched.

Tip Focaccia di Recco is best served hot from the oven, but in a pinch it can be kept in the fridge for a day or two and reheated in a preheated 250°F oven for 10 minutes.

Warm chickpea pancakes are a favorite beachside snack and aperitivo all along the Ligurian coastline and down into Tuscany. In Liguria, they are referred to as farinata *and are traditionally baked in wide, round copper pans in wood-fired ovens that can reach temperatures up to almost twice those of a home oven. At home, cooking times are lengthened and round cast-iron pans can be used, which will retain the heat and not warp. And don't forget to crack fresh black pepper on top before serving. It really livens up the flavor of the farinata. Serve with a dry white wine like Pigato from Liguria.*

CHICKPEA PANCAKE

·{ Makes **6** to **8** aperitivo servings }·

2 teaspoons fine sea salt

⅓ cup warm water

2½ cups cold water, plus more if needed

2¼ cups chickpea flour

¼ cup extra virgin olive oil, plus extra for greasing

Freshly ground black pepper

In a large bowl, stir the salt into the warm water to dissolve, then add the cold water. Gradually sift the chickpea flour into the water, whisking the batter continuously to avoid lumps. Once all the flour has been added, check to see that the consistency is that of milk. If necessary, add more cold water. Cover the bowl and set aside for at least 2 hours and up to 8 hours.

Preheat the oven to 500°F. Grease a 12- or 14-inch cast-iron pan or skillet with about a tablespoon of olive oil, then whisk the ¼ cup olive oil into the farinata batter.

Pour half the batter into the oiled pan, rotating the pan to equally distribute the batter. Bake for 20 to 25 minutes or until a golden crust has formed. If you like your farinata crispy, finish cooking it under the broiler until it blisters and black spots form.

Grind black pepper on top, cut the farinata into wedges, and serve hot.

To make a second farinata, whisk the batter well, as it tends to separate, then bake and serve as described above.

Chapter 2

MILAN

Nowhere in Italy has aperitivo, intended as both a drink and social exercise, caught on quite like in Milan. As soon as the business day draws to a close, locals take to rooftop bars and hotel lobbies to sip on the season's "it" cocktail and designer bar snacks made by the city's top chefs. It's tough to say what the Milanesi take most seriously: finance, footwear, or finger food.

Milan's aperitivo craze started back in the late nineties, when bar owners began setting up elaborate, all-you-can-eat spreads between the hours of six and nine p.m. The arrangement was that by spending a couple more euro for a cocktail or a glass of wine you were granted access to free food. A rip-off if you are on a liquid diet, but the best deal in town if you don't mind noshing at the bar. The aperitivo quickly became the focal point of a night out, and the *apericena* was born, an unfortunate compound word implying that dinner *(cena)* is replaced by aperitivo-hopping.

Recently there has been a return to a more civil approach to the aperitivo. Small, individual plates of food are brought to you directly, from the kitchen to the table. As the aperitivo scene continues to evolve, it's worth asking locals what's hot at the moment. In the selected guide at the back of this book (pages 214–216) you will find a list of time-tested aperitivo institutions as well as newcomers slated to last.

CAMPARI

Campari is just about as Italian as you get. Bright red in color and bracingly bitter in flavor, it stands out in a pack. It's the Ferrari of aperitivo liqueurs.

Intended to be sipped on its own or mixed into drinks by the ounce, Campari falls in the category of potable bitters, as opposed to aromatic or cocktail bitters such as Angostura. It's made by infusing a base of alcohol and water with a proprietary mix of herbs and fruits, including rhubarb, orange, and a variety of sour orange known as *chinotto* in Italian. The bitter infusion is then sweetened with sugar in the form of simple syrup and stiffened in accordance with its destination: 24% alcohol (48 proof) for American drinkers and 25% alcohol by volume (50 proof) for the Italians. Differences in taxation on alcohol are the most likely explanation, as Italians are not particularly well known for their high tolerances.

Campari's signature ruby red color comes from colorants. Until recently, Campari's colorant of choice was cochineal dye, an all-natural coloring agent extracted from a beetle-like insect native to Central and South America. In 2006, the beetle juice was replaced with FD&C Red #5. Some claim the change came in response to protests of animal rights activists, but it's more likely that the artificial colorant was simply less expensive.

History

Campari is the brainchild of Gaspare Campari. Born in 1828 in Cassolnovo, a small town outside Milan, Campari started working as a waiter and apprentice liquorist at the age of fourteen. He later was hired as *maître licoriste,* or master drink-maker, at Turin's renowned Del Cambio restaurant (see page 214). There, his regular customers included Vittorio Emmanuel, the first king of Italy, and Prime Minister Cavour. After a short stint in Novara, Campari moved to Milan in 1862 and purchased a bar of his own. There, he began tinkering with cordials and bitters, eventually stumbling upon a combination of botanicals that he first called *Bitter all'Uso d'Holanda,* or "in the style of Holland," based on his perceptions of Dutch liqueurs; this approximately a half century after the advent of sweet vermouth.

In order to get his red bitters in the hands of Milanese influencers, Campari moved his operation to the entrance of the newly inaugurated Galleria Vittorio Emanuele II (pictured opposite), an ice cube's toss from Milan's historic cathedral (pictured on page 66). Bar Campari, or Il Camparino, was soon *the* place to be and Campari's bitters *the* aperitivo of choice.

And if his bitters weren't enough to attract customers into his bar, Campari installed a revolutionary pumping system below the bar to bring icy-cold soda water directly to the counter: enter the Campari Soda.

There's no doubt that Campari passed down his astute business acumen to his youngest son, Davide, who is responsible for the world's first bottled cocktail: the Campari Soda.

Davide Campari was also the one to notice that neighboring bars had begun reselling Campari's signature bitters. He recognized the hidden opportunity and decided to grant other bar owners the right to buy and sell authentic Campari bitters in exchange for hanging a sign with Campari's name on it in their bars.

There are several alternatives to Campari, if you want to mix things up—just try these in the same quantities as you would Campari: Cappelletti, a more mellow, entryway bitter; Luxardo Bitter, with a taste like Campari, but with less zing and more orange peel; and Meletti, the most medicinal of the bunch. Cappelletti is the only one to use carmine (cochineal) as a natural, more traditional colorant.

CAMPARI ON THE ROCKS

Why mess with perfection?

---

2 ounces Campari

½ orange slice or lemon peel, optional

Fill a small chilled glass with 2 or 3 cubes of ice and pour the Campari on top. Garnish with the half slice of orange or lemon peel and serve.

CAMPARI SHAKERATO

Campari meets the cocktail shaker, both born in the mid-1900s.

---

2 ounces Campari

Put 3 ice cubes and the Campari in a cocktail shaker. Shake vigorously for a minute to break down the ice into tiny pieces. Pour into a chilled double shot glass or small martini glass.

CAMPARI SODA

Campari and soda water go together like Romeo and Giulietta.

2 ounces Campari
Soda water

Fill a rocks glass with 3 or 4 ice cubes. Add the Campari and top with the soda water.

Note You can do without the ice if you use chilled Campari and chilled soda water.

GARIBALDI

A classic aperitivo named after Giuseppe Garibaldi, the Italian general who assisted in the unification of Italy during the mid-nineteenth century. The Campari is a nod to Milan, as well as the red shirts worn by Garibaldi's military volunteers, while the orange juice symbolizes Garibaldi's arrival in Sicily, where oranges grow in abundance. Campari also pairs beautifully with grapefruit juice. To make a Campari Grapefruit, simply swap freshly squeezed grapefruit juice for the orange juice.

1½ ounces Campari
1½ ounces freshly squeezed
orange juice
Orange slice

Fill a rocks glass with 3 or 4 ice cubes. Add the Campari and orange juice and stir. Garnish with an orange slice.

CAMPARI ICE CUBES

*◦{ **Makes 14 (1-ounce) ice cubes** }◦*

A festive way to liven up tonic water or fruit juices, these bright red ice cubes also can be used to slowly transform a cocktail as the ice melts. Add Campari ice cubes to your next Manhattan and sip as it gradually becomes a Boulevardier.

4 ounces Campari

Stir together the Campari and 10 ounces water. Pour into a standard ice cube tray and freeze until frozen, 3 to 4 hours. Will keep indefinitely.

MI-TO

Born around 1870 with the arrival of Campari in Milan, this bittersweet aperitivo (pictured opposite) takes its name from the origins of its two ingredients: Campari from Milan and sweet vermouth from Torino.

1½ ounces Campari
1½ ounces sweet vermouth
½ slice orange, optional

Fill a rocks glass with 3 or 4 ice cubes. Add the Campari and vermouth, stir, and serve with a slice of orange, if desired.

In Italy, no two bartenders seem to agree upon how the Americano got its name. Some say the cocktail was christened in 1933 in honor of Primo "Americano" Carnera, the first Italian to win the World Heavyweight Boxing Championship in New York. Others claim it was what American ex-pats in Italy liked to drink during Prohibition. The most believable story is that the cocktail's name is a reference to the way in which it's prepared. Just as espresso watered down to American standards is called an Americano, a Mi-To mixed "in the American style," with ice and soda, goes by the same name.

AMERICANO

1 ounce Campari (see page 71)
1 ounce sweet vermouth
1 ounce soda water
Orange slice

Fill a rocks glass with 3 or 4 ice cubes. Add the Campari and vermouth, then top with the soda water. Garnish with the orange slice and serve.

My aperitivo table always includes a vegetable of some sort. This classic Italian recipe for raw vegetables paired with an olive oil–based sauce can be prepared year-round, but feel free to introduce additional seasonal vegetables like cherry tomatoes in the summer or endive leaves and cauliflower florets in the winter as they do at Milan's fashionable 10 Corso Como. Provide guests with individual bowls of the dipping sauce, keeping a little extra on hand in case they want more.

VEGETABLE PINZIMONIO

10 Corso Como

⋄{ Makes **6** to **8** aperitivo servings }⋄

3 carrots, quartered and cut into 3-inch-long sticks

3 stalks celery, cut into 3-inch-long sticks

12 radishes

1 medium fennel bulb, trimmed and cut lengthwise into ¼-inch-thick strips

1 cup extra virgin olive oil

¼ cup fresh lemon juice

1 tablespoon Dijon mustard

1½ teaspoons fine sea salt

Freshly ground black pepper

Arrange the vegetables on a large serving plate.

In a bowl, whisk together the olive oil, lemon juice, mustard, salt, and pepper to taste until emulsified. Divide the dipping sauce among six small bowls.

These crispy rice cakes are Milan's answer to leftover saffron risotto, as is the case at Ratanà, a modern trattoria serving a wide assortment of small plates referred to as rubitt *or "precious little things" in Milanese dialect. Some of these are pictured opposite, clockwise from top, including:* riso al salto; hand-chopped raw beef; fava bean puree; trout salad; gorgonzola, walnut, and honey crostino; mondeghili, *or Milanese fried meatballs; and spring pea and mint soup. Traditionally, riso al salto is slowly pan-fried over low heat, hence the name "al salto" from the verb "saltare" or to sauté. This technique results in a beautiful golden crust that can be recreated in the oven when preparing small individual patties for a group. The key to keeping the patties from falling apart is chilling the rice prior to baking so that it seizes up. Ideally, the risotto should be kept in the refrigerator overnight.*

RISO AL SALTO *Ratanà*

⊹{ **Makes 6 to 8 aperitivo servings** }⊹

6 cups chicken or beef broth, preferably homemade

3 tablespoons unsalted butter

2 tablespoons finely chopped onion

1½ cups Arborio or carnaroli rice

⅓ cup dry white wine

¼ teaspoon powdered saffron, or ⅓ teaspoon chopped saffron threads, dissolved or soaked in 1 cup hot broth

4 tablespoons freshly grated Parmigiano Reggiano

Freshly ground black pepper

Fine sea salt

1 large egg, beaten

Olive oil, for greasing

Bring the broth to a simmer in a large pot. In a separate large pot, heat 2 tablespoons of the butter and the onion over medium heat. Cook and stir until the onion is tender and translucent. Add the rice and stir. When the rice is well coated in butter and begins to crackle, increase the heat to high and pour in the wine. Continue stirring until the wine has evaporated.

Reduce the heat to medium and add ½ cup of the hot broth, stirring occasionally until the broth has been absorbed by the rice. Continue adding the broth about

continued —»

½ cup at a time, cooking until the broth has been absorbed and stirring from time to time so the rice doesn't stick to the pot. After about 15 minutes, add the saffron. Continue cooking, gradually adding the broth, until the rice is tender but firm to the bite and there is no more liquid in the pot.

Remove the pot from the heat and stir in the remaining 1 tablespoon butter, 2 tablespoons of the Parmigiano Reggiano, and a couple grindings of pepper. Taste and correct for salt.

Allow the risotto to come to room temperature, transfer to a bowl or container, cover, and refrigerate for at least 2 hours or overnight.

About 30 minutes before you plan to serve the rice patties, preheat the oven to 400°F. Remove the risotto from the refrigerator and stir in the beaten egg.

Grease two large baking sheets lightly with oil. Scoop ¼ cup risotto onto a baking sheet and flatten it into a 3-inch-wide and 1-inch-thick patty. A ring mold can also be used to shape the patties into perfect circles. Repeat, leaving at least 1 inch of space between each patty, until all the risotto has been shaped into patties. (You should have about 10 patties on each baking sheet.)

Bake for 10 minutes or until the edges of the rice patties are golden brown. Remove the pans from the oven and turn the patties over using a flat metal spatula. Dust the patties with the remaining 2 tablespoons Parmigiano Reggiano and return both pans to the top rack of the oven, if they will fit, otherwise finish cooking one at a time. Broil for about 8 minutes. Let cool for at least 5 minutes before serving.

Risotto cakes can be served warm or at room temperature.

In Italy, wasting food could arguably be classified as the eighth deadly sin. Should an Italian cook end up with leftover mashed potatoes, croquettes are their salvation. A simple squeeze of lemon will leave your guests wondering about your secret ingredient, as well as coming back for more.

LEMON POTATO CROQUETTES

·{ Makes 6 to 8 aperitivo servings }·

4 cups mashed potatoes

2 tablespoons grated Parmigiano Reggiano

2 teaspoons lemon zest

1 tablespoon fresh lemon juice

Fine sea salt

Freshly ground black pepper

1 cup all-purpose flour

2 large eggs

1½ cups fine breadcrumbs

Oil for frying

In a large bowl, mix the mashed potatoes with the grated Parmigiano Reggiano, lemon zest, and lemon juice; season with salt and pepper.

In a shallow bowl, stir together the flour, a pinch of salt, and a couple grindings of pepper; in a second shallow bowl, whisk together the eggs with a tablespoon of water; place the breadcrumbs in a third shallow bowl.

Form the potato mixture into 2 by ¾-inch logs. Roll the logs in the flour, shaking off the excess, dip in the egg wash, then roll in the breadcrumbs to coat. Heat 1½ inches of oil in a shallow heavy-bottomed pan over medium-high heat. You can test if the oil is hot enough for frying by dropping a cube of bread in the oil. It should sizzle and float to the top immediately.

Fry the croquettes in batches until golden brown on all sides, about 1 minute per batch, turning halfway through cooking time. Drain on paper towels and serve warm.

*While making a Negroni (page 120) on a busy night, the owner of Milan's Bar Basso reached for the gin and came up with sparkling wine. After scolding the bar back for mixing up the bottles, he tasted the mistaken cocktail only to discover he'd come up with a simple, super-drinkable twist on a classic: the Negroni Sbagliato (*sbagliato *is Italian for "mistaken").*

NEGRONI SBAGLIATO
Bar Basso

1½ ounces Campari (see page 71)

1½ ounces sweet vermouth

1½ ounces dry sparkling wine, such as a dry Prosecco

Orange slice

Fill a rocks glass with 3 or 4 ice cubes. Add the Campari and vermouth, then stir with a bar spoon. Top with the sparkling wine and stir again. Garnish with the orange slice.

Bar Basso

Bar Basso (pictured opposite and on following pages) is a Milan institution. During the city's annual Salone del Mobile design fair or any given fashion week, the wood-paneled dive is packed with stylish insiders sipping cocktails well into the night. The bar's owner, Mirko Stocchetto, revolutionized the way people drink in Milan. Once the resident barman at Hotel Monaco in Venice and later at Hotel de la Poste in Cortina, Stocchetto took over Bar Basso in 1967, introducing American-style cocktails that were formerly only to be found in hotel bars. His libations served in custom-designed glassware didn't go unnoticed. How could they? Negronis are poured over a Rubik's-size ice cube and served in a glass chalice that could pass for a stemmed fishbowl, requiring two hands to drink. Thankfully, Sbagliatos come in a more manageable glass, often leading one to order a second. Today, Bar Basso is run by Stocchetto's son Maurizio (pictured on following page), whose contagious smile is a welcome sight during the long, gray Milan winters.

The Navigli neighborhood surrounding Milan's canals has become a sort of restaurant row, where the action starts with the aperitivo and continues long into the night. Taglio, a friendly restaurant, bar, and food shop, serves these savory stuffed mussels from time to time. They make great party fare because they are simple to prepare and can be eaten easily with one's hands. Pair with a dry white wine or an Italian variation of the Gin and Tonic (pages 107 and 111).

BAKED MUSSELS WITH SPICY MAYONNAISE

Taglio

⋅{ **Makes 6 to 8 aperitivo servings** }⋅

2 pounds mussels, scrubbed and beards removed

1 cup panko breadcrumbs

2 teaspoons minced garlic

¼ cup fresh flat-leaf parsley leaves, finely chopped

3 tablespoons extra virgin olive oil

2 tablespoons grated Parmigiano Reggiano

½ cup Italian-style mayonnaise, (see page 200) or store-bought

1 teaspoon fresh ginger juice (pass peeled ginger through juicer or buy 100% natural ginger juice)

½ teaspoon mustard powder

Preheat the oven to 400°F. Place the mussels in a wide pot, cover, and set over high heat. Check frequently and remove the mussels as they open. (Toss out any mussels that do not open.) Discard the empty half shell from each mussel and arrange the opened mussels on a large baking sheet. Filter the liquid remaining in the pot through cheesecloth and set aside.

In a bowl, mix together the panko, garlic, parsley, 2 tablespoons of the olive oil, and the grated cheese. Add a tablespoon of the

mussel cooking liquid for flavor and to further bind the stuffing. Fill the shells with the stuffing and arrange on a baking sheet. Bake for 5 minutes until the stuffing is hot and lightly browned.

Meanwhile, whisk together the mayonnaise, remaining 1 tablespoon olive oil, ginger juice, and mustard powder until thoroughly blended.

Remove the mussels from the oven and serve warm with a small dollop of spicy mayonnaise on top of each.

When the Italian fashion brand Trussardi opened their sprawling flagship store across from La Scala, Milan's historic opera house, they strategically included a ground-floor café to revitalize weary shoppers. As any serious fashionista knows, nothing helps one pull the trigger when wavering over a new handbag or pair of cufflinks like a little liquid encouragement. At Trussardi Café (pictured on page 96), bartender Tommaso Cecca has not only transformed the brand's fragrances into aromatic cocktails, but made his own twists on Italian classics, such as the Americano (page 76). Replacing soda water with a beer float makes for a frothy, refreshing cocktail (pictured opposite). For a lighter, more floral version of this cocktail Cecca uses dry white vermouth, Weizen or wheat beer, and a lemon peel as garnish. To achieve Trussardi-worthy froth at home, try using an Aerolatte, a mini whisk-blender more commonly used to prepare milk foam for a cappuccino.

BEER AMERICANO

Trussardi Café

1½ ounces Campari (see page 71)

1½ ounces sweet vermouth, preferably Carpano Antica Formula

3 ounces lager

Orange zest, for garnish

Combine the Campari, vermouth, and 6 ice cubes (see Note) in a tall tumbler or Burgundy wine glass. Stir with a bar spoon to chill. Pour the lager into a separate glass and whip the beer into a foam using an Aerolatte or immersion blender. Top the cocktail with beer foam and finish with orange zest.

Note Consider replacing traditional ice cubes with one large sphere or square cube. Statement ice molds can be purchased online. Look for Tovolo brand molds, which are easy to use.

I first discovered Giacomo Bistrot (pictured opposite and page 94) as a graduate student in Milan. The marble-clad bar room has an old-world charm that I couldn't resist. I would go in for dinner from time to time, but the real draws are the small plates of savory nibbles always served with cocktails at the bar. My favorite are these irresistible tempura-style fried vegetables, which are also prepared at their sister restaurant, Giacomo Arengario (pictured on page 66), located inside the Museo del Novecento with bird's-eye views of the Duomo.

FRIED SHOESTRING VEGETABLES *Giacomo Bistrot*

⊰{ **Makes 6 to 8 aperitivo servings** }⊱

1 waxy potato, peeled and shredded or julienned (about 1 cup)

3 carrots, shredded or julienned (about 1 cup)

2 zucchini, shredded or julienned (about 1 cup)

1 cup rice flour

½ cup all-purpose flour

½ cup cold sparkling water

3 cups oil for frying

Fine sea salt

Toss the potato, carrots, and zucchini together in a bowl.

In a separate bowl, stir the rice and all-purpose flours together and slowly incorporate the cold water. Place the bowl of batter in an ice bath to keep it chilled.

Heat 2 inches of the oil in a shallow heavy-bottomed pan over medium heat.

When the oil is hot enough (see instructions page 83), use tongs to dip tablespoon-size clumps of vegetables into the batter. Allow the excess batter to drip off before lowering the vegetables into the hot oil.

Fry the vegetables for a couple of minutes per side, or until golden brown. Transfer to paper towels to drain and dust with salt. Repeat with the remaining vegetables and serve hot.

Shop and Serve

>|< Not all aperitivo spreads require cooking. Invest a little time and money in stocking your pantry with quality Italian ingredients, and you will always be ready when friends stop by at the last minute.

> OLIVES

Imported Italian olives are an obvious choice for an aperitivo and for good reason; they are tasty and easy to serve. Italy is home to over fifty olive varieties, some of which are best cured and others that are better off pressed and used to make oil. Three excellent table varieties that can be found abroad are small *cailletier* olives, known as Niçoise when they come from around Nice and Taggiasca when they come from Liguria; bright green *nocellara del belice* olives from Castelvetrano in Sicily; and huge, buttery olives from Cerignola in Puglia. When buying olives, look for tight skins and firm flesh. If possible, ask to sample a couple of different varieties to make sure you buy olives that are to your liking. Store olives in a cool place, outside the refrigerator for a couple of weeks. They should be kept in their brine, or rinsed and covered with olive oil.

> NUTS

Sicily is home to some of the best nuts in the world: broad, flat Pizzuta almonds from outside Avola and Bronte pistachios grown at the base of Mount Etna. The oils in nuts have a tendency to go rancid if stored improperly. Keep shelled nuts in opaque, airtight containers in the refrigerator. Nuts can also be stored in the freezer, if you buy in bulk.

> SALUMI

Italy is home to hundreds of different cured meats, or salumi, the large majority of which are made from her majesty, the pig. Some are salt-cured, like prosciutto crudo, others are smoked, such as speck and varieties of pancetta, while others still have been preserved in fat. Next time you visit a specialty Italian food store or well-stocked grocery store, purchase a couple to taste at home so you know what to buy for your next aperitivo party. Mortadella can be easily cut into cubes, while salumi with casings should be sliced with the casings removed—a small favor for your guests.

No visit to Milan is complete without a veal cutlet. Dipped in beaten egg, covered with breadcrumbs, and fried in butter, a single costoletta alla Milanese *(or "rib chop in the style of Milan") can often fill an entire plate. Small bone-in lamb chops can easily be prepared in the same way and make for an excellent* aperitivo, *particularly because they can be prepared ahead of time and served at room temperature.*

LAMB CHOPS ALLA MILANESE

‧{ Makes **6** to **8** aperitivo servings }‧

18 small lamb rib chops, bone-in
1 cup all-purpose flour
2 large eggs
1 cup fine breadcrumbs

¼ cup grated Parmigiano Reggiano
8 tablespoons (1 stick) unsalted butter, for frying
Flaky sea salt, such as Maldon

Using a pair of kitchen scissors, remove the thick layer of fat from around the edge of each chop, being careful to maintain the medallion shape of the chop.

Place the chops between two sheets of plastic wrap and flatten until ¼ inch thick.

Put the flour in a shallow bowl; in another shallow bowl, whisk together the eggs and 1 tablespoon water; and in a third shallow bowl, mix the breadcrumbs and grated Parmigiano Reggiano. Dredge each chop in the flour, shaking off the excess. Dip in the egg wash and then press both sides into the breadcrumbs.

In a heavy skillet, heat 2 tablespoons of the butter over medium-high heat until the foaming subsides. Working in batches of 4 or 5 chops to avoid overcrowding and adding 2 tablespoons of butter before each batch, cook the chops for about 3 minutes per side. They should be golden brown and crunchy on the outside and tender pink in the center. As they finish cooking, transfer the chops to a platter, sprinkle a little salt on each chop, and wrap a 1-inch-wide strip of aluminum foil around the end of each bone, so they can be eaten with one's hands without making a mess. Serve warm.

Bartender Guglielmo Miriello of Dry (see page 105) has made a name for himself serving forgotten cocktails like the Hanky Panky, a combination of gin, vermouth, and Fernet Branca created in the early 1900s at London's Hotel Savoy. In his Vintage Negroni, Miriello tries to re-create the flavor of what the first sweet vermouths may have tasted like by adding Barolo Chinato, the celebrated Piedmontese wine fortified and aromatized in the style of vermouth, but with a distinctly bitter note of quinine bark. Barolo Chinato can be found in most specialty wine stores, while mandarin or orange bitters will require a trip to a liquor store or quick search on the web.

VINTAGE NEGRONI

Dry

¾ ounce Campari (see page 71)
¾ ounce sweet vermouth
¾ ounce London dry gin
½ ounce Barolo Chinato
1 dash mandarin bitters or orange bitters
Orange slice

Fill a mixing glass with 3 or 4 ice cubes. Stir to chill the glass, then pour off the water. Add the Campari, vermouth, gin, chinato, and bitters to the mixing glass and stir to chill for 15 seconds. Fill a rocks glass with 3 ice cubes and strain the Negroni over the ice. Garnish with the orange slice.

FOCACCIA

Freshly baked focaccia is a building block for many great aperitivi. The soft, supple flat-bread can be served on its own, topped with endless combinations of ingredients, or stuffed to make mini sandwiches. Don't be discouraged if your first attempts end up recycled into breadcrumbs or even tossed in the trash; getting to know dough comes with practice. Check on the dough as it rises to make sure it has doubled in size before you stretch it out or shape it. If possible, place dough to rise in a 1- or 2-quart glass measuring cup or bowl, covered with plastic wrap. This way you will be able to easily track the dough's volume. The time required to achieve this will vary based on temperature, humidity, and the quality of the yeast you use. Once you master the basics of rising and baking homemade focaccia, you won't go back to store-bought. The sweet aroma that fills your kitchen is worth the effort alone.

BASIC FOCACCIA DOUGH

∘{ Makes 28 ounces dough }∘

4 cups all-purpose flour or Italian 00 flour, plus more for dusting

2 teaspoons active dry yeast, or 1½ teaspoons instant yeast (see Note)

2 teaspoons fine sea salt

1¼ cups warm water, plus more if needed

2 tablespoons extra virgin olive oil, plus extra for greasing

To make the dough by hand: In a large bowl, combine the flour, yeast, and salt. Add the warm water and the olive oil and stir with a wooden spoon until the dough comes together. If necessary, add more warm water, a teaspoon at a time. Shape the dough into a ball and transfer to a floured work surface.

Knead the dough until it is smooth and elastic, about 10 minutes. To knead the dough, push it down and stretch it back and forth with the heels of your hands. Then push the dough back into a ball, rotate, and repeat.

To make the dough in a stand mixer: In the bowl of a stand mixer fitted with the dough hook, combine the flour, yeast, salt, and warm water and mix on low speed for 2 minutes. If the dough doesn't come together and separate from the walls of the mixer bowl, add more warm water, a teaspoon at a time. Add the olive oil. Increase the speed to medium and beat until the dough is smooth and elastic, 3 to 4 minutes.

Once the dough has been properly kneaded, shape it into a ball and place it in a lightly greased medium glass bowl or 1- or 2-quart glass measuring cup. Cover with plastic wrap and set aside in a warm place. Allow the dough to rise until it has doubled in size. This can take anywhere from 30 minutes to over an hour.

Now the dough is ready to be rolled out into one large focaccia or divided and shaped into smaller *focaccette*.

Note Instant yeast is extremely convenient, needs no proofing, and results in bread with lots of inherent taste. My favorite brand is SAF, which is available on Amazon. The more common active dry yeast is only 75 percent as powerful.

ROSEMARY AND OLIVE FOCACCIA

֍{ **Makes 6 to 8 aperitivo servings** }֍

---

1 (28-ounce) ball Basic Focaccia Dough (page 100)

All-purpose flour, for dusting

2 tablespoons extra virgin olive oil

¼ cup pitted olives

1 tablespoon finely chopped fresh rosemary, or 1 teaspoon dried rosemary

Flaky sea salt, such as Maldon

Turn out the dough onto a lightly floured work surface. Roll the dough into a large rectangle, approximately 18 by 13 inches. Carefully transfer the dough to a large, greased or parchment paper–lined baking sheet of the same size. Spread the dough across the pan until it reaches the edges, pulling on it gently with your hands. Brush the surface with the olive oil, arrange the olives across the top, and sprinkle with the rosemary. Cover with plastic wrap or a clean kitchen towel and let the dough rise for 45 minutes.

About 15 minutes before you're ready to bake, preheat the oven to 350°F. Bake the focaccia for 20 to 25 minutes or until golden brown but still pretty soft. Transfer the pan to a rack to cool. Finish the focaccia with flaky sea salt. Serve warm or at room temperature. Cut into squares using a serrated bread knife.

Tucked away inside the courtyard of an eighteenth-century urban farmhouse, Un Posto a Milano, is the place to go in Milan for a taste of country life. Chef Nicola Cavallaro diligently sources ingredients from sustainable farms located just outside the city and, every Tuesday, invites a producer or farmer to join him and the team behind the bar for a farm-to-table aperitivo. Cavallaro uses soft whole-wheat flour ground by Mulino Marino to make his focaccia. In terms of flavor, you may find a mix of whole-grain flour and all-purpose works best. Serve the focaccia at room temperature along with a Posto Punch (page 114).

Un Posto a Milano

WHOLE WHEAT AND POTATO FOCACCIA

>{ **Makes 6 to 8 aperitivo servings** }·

2 teaspoons active dry yeast, or 1½ teaspoons instant yeast (see Note, page 101)

½ cup warm water, plus more if needed

4 cups whole wheat, farro, or spelt flour, possibly mixed with all-purpose

2 cups mashed potatoes

2 teaspoons fine sea salt

¾ cup milk

¼ cup olive oil, plus extra for greasing and brushing

1 cup thinly sliced vegetables (such as onions, potatoes, tomatoes, peppers, fennel), optional

1 teaspoon flaky sea salt, such as Maldon

In a small bowl or glass measuring cup, stir the yeast into the warm water until dissolved.

In a large bowl or the bowl of a stand mixer, mix the flour, mashed potatoes, and fine sea salt. Gradually add the milk, olive oil, and the yeast mixture. Knead by hand for about 8 minutes or on low speed with the dough hook for about 4 minutes, until the dough is elastic but still slightly sticky. If necessary, gradually add more warm water, a teaspooon at a time. Cover and let rise in a warm place until doubled in volume, about 45 minutes.

Turn the dough out onto a large, lightly greased or parchment paper–lined baking sheet. Spread the dough across the pan until it reaches the edges, then brush the surface with olive oil. Cover with

continued —»

plastic wrap or a clean kitchen towel and let rise for 45 minutes. The dough should be puffy.

About 15 minutes before you're ready to bake, preheat the oven to 350°F. Just before baking, dimple the dough with your fingers. If you're using sliced vegetables, gently distribute them on top of the focaccia.

Bake for 20 to 25 minutes or until the focaccia is golden brown but still pretty soft. Transfer the pan to a rack to cool. Finish the focaccia with flaky sea salt. Serve warm or at room temperature. Cut into small squares using a bread knife.

Princi Bakery

The once unheard of combination of cocktails and pizza is gaining a following in cosmopolitan Milan in large part thanks to Dry, a bar/pizzeria in Milan's trendy Brera district. Bartender Guliermo Miriello pours updated versions of classic cocktails to go with the focaccias of chef Simone Lombardi (pictured on page 108), served in the front bar area, and pizzas, served in the back. Since opening, the focaccia with vitello tonnato and caper powder (pictured center on page 109) has been a constant on the bar menu, and for good reason. While making your own caper powder may prove difficult, or at least time consuming, without a dehydrator, finely chopped capers are a good stand-in. Good-quality store-bought focaccia can also be topped with vitello tonnato.

FOCACCIA WITH VITELLO TONNATO AND CAPERS

◊{ **Makes 6 to 8 aperitivo servings** }◊

1½ to 2 pounds lean veal roast, preferably top round

1 carrot

1 stalk celery

1 onion

3 sprigs fresh parsley

1 dried bay leaf

1 (28-ounce) ball Basic Focaccia Dough (page 100)

1 (7-ounce) can tuna packed in olive oil

¼ cup extra virgin olive oil, plus more for serving

1 teaspoon fresh lemon juice, plus more if needed

1 cup mayonnaise, Italian-style (see page 200) or store-bought

½ cup salt-packed capers, soaked, rinsed, and finely chopped in a food processor (see page 14)

Put the veal, carrot, celery, onion, parsley, and bay leaf in a medium pot; add enough water to cover, then remove the veal and set it aside. Bring the water to a boil and return the meat to the pot.

Once the water returns to a boil, reduce the heat to maintain a simmer, cover the pot, and cook for 2 hours. Remove the pot from the heat and let the meat cool in its broth.

continued —»

MILAN

Meanwhile, divide the focaccia dough into four 7-ounce balls and stretch to fit four 8-inch round baking dishes, or place the four disks on two baking sheets. Cover with plastic wrap and allow the dough to rest in a warm spot until it doubles in volume and becomes airy, at least 45 minutes.

About 20 minutes before you're ready to bake, preheat the oven to 400°F.

Drain the canned tuna and put it into a food processor with the olive oil and lemon juice. Process until blended uniformly, then fold into the mayonnaise. Adjust the flavors, adding more lemon juice for tartness if needed.

Once the veal has cooled, transfer it to a cutting board (reserve the broth for another use) and thinly slice. If you have a meat slicer, use it.

Arrange two of the pans of focaccia dough on a baking sheet and place the baking sheet on the lowest oven rack. If not using pans, place one baking sheet directly on the lowest oven rack.

Bake for about 10 minutes or until the focaccias just begin to turn golden. Remove from the oven and turn out onto a rack to cool. Bake and cool the remaining two focaccias in the same way.

Once cool enough to handle, cut each focaccia into eight pieces. Place a tablespoon of tuna sauce on the center of each slice of focaccia. Arrange a slice of veal on top and finish with a pinch of chopped capers and a drizzle of olive oil.

Variations

PROSCIUTTO AND STRACCIATELLA FOCACCIA
(pictured top on page 109)
Top each slice of focaccia with a spoonful of creamy stracciatella cheese and a half-slice of paper-thin prosciutto crudo. Stracciatella are tangy, cream-soaked strands of mozzarella. Look for it at specialty cheese stores or substitute with burrata.

STRACCHINO, MORTADELLA, AND WATERCRESS-STUFFED
FOCACCIA (pictured left on page 109)
Before cutting each focaccia into eight wedges, cut the bread in half horizontally. Spread creamy stracchino cheese across the bottom half of each focaccia. Top with a handful of watercress, then fold thinly sliced mortadella across the cress.

At Rebelot, a small restaurant located along Milan's main canal, globetrotting bartender Oscar Quagliarini helped put together a cocktail program to complement the kitchen's upbeat small-plate menu. My favorite of his many "Gintos" calls for No. 209, a citrus-forward gin distilled in San Francisco, and Thomas Henry tonic water from Germany, finished with small fresh chili peppers and a sprig of rosemary. If you can't find No. 209, look for another citrusy gin like Bluecoat rather than a more classic juniper-driven London dry.

CHILI PEPPER AND ROSEMARY GIN TONIC

Rebelot

1½ ounces No. 209 gin

3 to 4 ounces Thomas Henry tonic water or other quality tonic water (see Note)

5 small fresh red chili peppers

1 sprig fresh rosemary

Fill a tall, narrow Collins glass with 4 ice cubes. Add the gin, then the tonic water and chili peppers. Stir well and garnish with the rosemary.

Note Nowadays, not all tonic waters are made the same. For a cleaner flavor, look for brands that contain real quinine rather than artificial flavors and that are sweetened with natural cane sugar and not high-fructose corn syrup.

Each spring, interior designers and architects flock to Milan to attend the city's Salone del Mobile, a weeklong design fair featuring both established and new talent from around the world. These prosciutto-wrapped vegetables were part of a swanky spread served at a design show inside Palazzo Clerici, a seventeenth-century beauty in the center of town. The vegetables and pesto can be prepped ahead of time and stored in the fridge. Ideally, prosciutto crudo—cured, ready-to-eat ham—should be purchased the day of and kept at room temperature. If purchased ahead of time, be sure to bring the prosciutto up to room temperature before wrapping the vegetables to really enjoy its salty-sweet flavor.

PROSCIUTTO-WRAPPED VEGETABLES

⊳{ **Makes 6 to 8 aperitivo servings** }⊲

½ cup loosely packed fresh basil leaves

¼ cup fresh mint leaves

¼ cup raw almonds

1 tablespoon olive oil

1 teaspoon fresh lemon juice

¼ teaspoon fine sea salt, plus more if needed

18 slices prosciutto crudo (about 7 ounces)

1 carrot, cut into 3 x ¼-inch sticks

1 stalk celery, cut into 3 x ¼-inch sticks

1 zucchini, cut into 3 x ¼-inch sticks

1 medium fennel bulb, cut lengthwise into ½-inch-thick pieces

In a food processor, blend the basil, mint, almonds, olive oil, lemon juice, and salt until smooth. Taste and adjust the salt.

Working in batches, arrange slices of prosciutto across a flat surface without overlapping them. Spread a teaspoon of the basil-mint pesto vertically across one end of each slice. Layer a stick of each vegetable—carrot, celery, zucchini, and fennel—on top of the pesto. Beginning with the pesto end, roll the entire slice of prosciutto around the vegetables. Repeat with the remaining prosciutto, pesto, and vegetable sticks. Arrange on a platter and serve at room temperature.

At Fioraio Bianchi, a small café housed inside an exquisite florist shop, gin is taken seriously and served simply. Gin Mare, a gin from Barcelona that's infused with Italian basil, Greek thyme, Turkish rosemary, and Spanish olives, is paired with tonic water and a slice of fennel. A truly Mediterranean take on a British standard.

FENNEL GIN AND TONIC

Fioraio Bianchi Caffè

1½ ounces Gin Mare

3 to 4 ounces quality tonic water (see Note, page 107)

Fennel slice

Fill a rocks glass with 3 or 4 ice cubes. Add the gin, then the tonic water. Stir and garnish with the slice of fennel.

Aimo Moroni, the chef-owner of Milan's Il Luogo di Aimo e Nadia, has a fine-tuned sensibility for sourcing the most flavorful ingredients Italy has to offer. His oregano isn't just any oregano. It's grown in a nature reserve on Sicily's eastern coast. His tomatoes? Still warm from the sun shining over Pachino. When preparing panzanella, the classic bread-and-tomato salad of his native Tuscany, Moroni inevitably uses the best produce and products available. Take inspiration from Moroni and select your ingredients with care. You'll be amazed how delicious simple tastes. And to give this dish a touch of sophistication, the ingredients are pulsed into small pieces, distinguishing the salad from its more rustic origins. Prepare this dish a couple of days before serving as the flavor improves over time. Bring up to room temperature to serve.

PANZANELLA MILANESE

Il Luogo di Aimo e Nadia

→{ Makes **6 to 8** aperitivo servings }←

3 ounces stale rustic Italian bread, torn into small pieces

¼ fresh cherry or grape tomato juice (see juicing instructions, page 193)

1 cup diced carrot

1 cup diced cherry or grape tomatoes

1 cup diced celery hearts

½ cup diced spring onions

1 tablespoon salt-packed capers, rinsed and chopped

3 fresh basil leaves, chopped

¼ cup extra virgin olive oil, plus more for serving

1 teaspoon white wine vinegar

Flaky sea salt, such as Maldon

In a large bowl, place the bread and soften with the tomato juice and ¼ cup water. Add the diced vegetables, capers, basil, olive oil, and vinegar. Toss and add salt to taste. Transfer to a food processor and pulse until the ingredients have been reduced to tiny pieces. Cover with a kitchen towel and set aside for at least 2 hours so the bread soaks up the juices. Serve in small bowls and finish with a drizzle of olive oil.

Bulgari Hotel —»

Bartender Andrea Aquino is the author of Un Posto a Milano's signature nonalcoholic aperitivo. His recipe calls for red currant juice, but pure pomegranate juice lends this version a similar flavor and striking color.

POSTO PUNCH

Un Posto a Milano

1 cardamom seed

3 teaspoons sugar

1 ounce fresh lemon juice

2 ounces pure pomegranate juice, chilled

2 ounces apple juice, chilled

1 sprig fresh rosemary

Crush the cardamom seed with the sugar in a mortar and pestle. In a cocktail shaker, combine the cardamom sugar with the lemon, pomegranate, and apple juices and shake well. Pour into a rocks glass filled with 3 or 4 ice cubes and garnish with the rosemary.

Nonalcoholic Aperitivi

Most café menus in Italy have a section dedicated to *aperitivi analcolici*, nonalcoholic options. Sparkling sodas such as Gingerino and Sanbittèr are the most bitter and recall the flavor of Campari. Then there is Crodino, a navel orange–colored aperitivo that is slightly less aggressive in flavor, but still has an aftertaste of pine. San Pellegrino, Italy's largest bottled water producer, has a line of citrus flavored sparkling waters that range from the more common *aranciata* (orange) and *limonata* (lemon) to *pompelmo* (grapefruit) and *melograno* (pomegranate). Other Italian classics include citron-based Tassoni Cedrata (see page 43) and chinotto (see page 57).

{ farther afield }

FLORENCE

Chicken liver crostini are truly Tuscan. Every time I see them on a menu or prepare them at home, I am transported back to the musky cellar of a Tuscan winemaker whose mother served me life-changing chicken liver pâté, slightly sweet with a deep, dark, complex flavor that has become my gold standard. Tuscan cooks typically use wine to deglaze the pan. But when I found myself in a pinch once, I used sweet vermouth instead and discovered I enjoy the added sweetness.

CHICKEN LIVER CROSTINI

›{ Makes **4** to **6** aperitivo servings }‹

8 ounces chicken livers

Fine sea salt and freshly ground black pepper

2 tablespoons unsalted butter

3 tablespoons extra virgin olive oil

¾ cup finely chopped onion

1 fresh sage sprig

1 fresh rosemary sprig

1 salted anchovy fillet, rinsed and minced

1 teaspoon salted capers, rinsed and chopped

2 tablespoons sweet vermouth

1 teaspoon fresh lemon juice

12 crostini (see recipe page 185)

Rinse the livers under cold running water and pat dry with paper towels. Remove any fat or veins, season with salt and pepper, and set aside.

In a large skillet, heat the butter and 1 tablespoon of the olive oil over medium heat. Once the butter has melted, add the onion, sage, and rosemary and season with salt and pepper. Cook, stirring occasionally, until the onion softens and begins to brown, about 5 minutes. Add the anchovy and capers, reduce the heat to medium-low, and cook for 5 minutes more. Transfer the onion mixture to a bowl, remove and discard the herbs, then wipe the skillet clean.

Return the skillet to high heat. Once hot, add the remaining 2 tablespoons olive oil. Place the livers in the pan in a single layer; do not overcrowd the pan. Cook without moving until the

continued —»

livers are nicely browned, about 2 minutes, then flip and brown the opposite side for another minute.

Return the onion mixture to the pan with the livers, then add the vermouth and lemon juice. Raise the heat to high, stir to deglaze for 30 seconds, then remove the pan from the heat. Cool the liver mixture to room temperature.

Once cool, pulse the liver mixture in a food processor until it is fairly smooth. Season with salt and pepper to taste and serve spread across the crostini.

Note Chicken liver pâté can be stored in the fridge for up to a week. Double the recipe and keep some on hand for impromptu aperitivo parties, making sure to bring the pâté to room temperature before serving.

The best aperitivi I have ever had in Florence were in the home of American food writer Faith Willinger, who has lived and cooked in Italy for over forty years, traveling the country far and wide in search of the best ingredients. Her kitchen is a true treasure trove of Italian delights, which she draws from to prepare small dishes to serve to her guests. She refers to these preparations as cazzatine, *loosely translated as "little nothings," and they can vary from grilled bread drizzled with excellent olive oil, known as* fett'unta, *or leftover cauliflower stems boiled and pureed into a cream. Her Tuscan kale chips are simply irresistible and predate the American kale obsession by decades. She prepares her chips in a cast-iron pan, but I have found crisping them in the oven works well too and frees up the stove for preparing other little nothings.*

TUSCAN KALE CHIPS

⊹{ **Makes 6 to 8 aperitivo servings** }⊹

24 large Tuscan (lacinato) kale leaves

2 tablespoons extra virgin olive oil

2 teaspoons fine sea salt

Freshly ground black pepper

Preheat the oven to 250°F. Slice the kale leaves lengthwise on either side of the center rib. Remove the ribs and slice the laeves into 2-inch-wide squares. In a large bowl, toss the kale with the olive oil, salt, and a couple grindings of pepper. Arrange the kale in a single layer on two baking sheets. Bake until crisp, 30 to 35 minutes. Transfer the kale chips to a wire rack to cool. The chips can be made in advance and stored in an airtight container for up to 2 days.

NEGRONI

The Negroni is Italy's greatest contribution to the cocktail world. Personally, I would argue that it is one of Italy's greatest contributions to the world in general, right up there with the Coliseum and the Vespa.

While nothing beats a Bellini on a lazy June afternoon in Venice, the Negroni is strong enough to stand up to a Boston snowstorm and refreshing enough to handle the Texas heat in August. Made with equal parts gin, Campari, and sweet vermouth, it's a dark, bittersweet blend that can match many moods.

The drink is named after Count Camillo Negroni, who inherited his taste for gin from his English mother on his many trips to London. As the story goes, the cocktail Negroni was created in 1919 in Florence by Fosco Scarelli, the then bartender of Caffè Casoni, which was later moved and renamed Caffè Giacosa. Count Negroni was a Casoni regular, allowing Scarelli to get to know him, and his wife, quite well. Apparently the countess wasn't particularly pleased with her husband's drinking.

So as a seasoned professional, Scarelli fulfilled and, more important, said nothing of the count's request to replace the water in his Americano (page 76) with gin, London dry of course. Other Casoni clients caught on to the count's trick and began ordering their Americanos Negroni-style. To an untrained eye, the drinks look identical and in order to distinguish them, Scarelli would add a whole slice of orange to an Americano and just a half slice to a Negroni, a subtle gesture worthy of a count.

NEGRONI

1¼ ounces London dry gin
1¼ ounces Campari (see page 71)
1¼ ounces sweet vermouth
½ orange slice

Fill a mixing glass with ice, add the gin, Campari, and vermouth, and stir with a bar spoon. Strain into a rocks glass filled with 3 or 4 ice cubes. Garnish with the half slice of orange.

Note on vermouth Most bars in Italy use a basic sweet vermouth like Martini & Rossi for Negronis. If you are looking for something with a clean, smooth flavor, try Cocchi Vermouth di Torino. And for a more complex, herbal Negroni, try Carpano Antica Formula or Punt e Mes.

Note on ice While Negronis are commonly served up in a martini glass in swanky American cocktail bars, they are always served on the rocks in Italy. That is, unless you come across a bartender who has spent some time abroad.

Note on flamed garnishes For a more modern take on the orange garnish, use a paring knife to cut an oval strip of orange zest. Using your thumb and index finger, hold the short side of the peel over the glass. In your opposite hand, light a match and place it between the orange peel and the glass. Gently start to pinch the edges of the peel together, then fold it in half entirely. This quick movement will release the essential oils in the orange peel and spray them across the flame and into your drink. You can use the same technique with other citrus peels, like lemon and grapefruit, in order to enhance their aroma.

NEGRONI: VARIATIONS ON A THEME

While the classic Negroni recipe calls for equal parts gin, Campari, and sweet vermouth, it's believed that Negroni himself would have been served a more vermouth-heavy cocktail. Recently, bartenders in Italy and beyond have begun playing around with proportions and ingredients. Feel free to do so as well. Here are some suggestions for where to begin.

	Spirit	*Bitter*	*Sweet*
Negroni	Gin	Campari (see page 71)	Sweet vermouth
Negroni Sbagliato	Dry sparkling wine	Campari	Sweet vermouth
Negrosky	Vodka	Campari	Sweet vermouth
Boulevardier	Bourbon	Campari	Sweet vermouth
Mexican Negroni	Mescal	Campari	Sweet vermouth
Marsala Negroni	Gin	Campari	Sweet Marsala
Negroni Bianco	Gin	Cocchi Americano (see page 35)	Splash of maraschino
Rhubarb Negroni	Gin	Dry vermouth	Rabarbaro Zucca (see page 51)

Chapter 3

PADUA

Padua is a small town of about 200,000 residents in northeastern Italy that attracts busloads of tourists daily who come to see Giotto's colorful frescos in the Scrovegni chapel, to tour St. Anthony's Basilica, and pray in front of the saint's tongue, on display as a large golden relic, and end their day with a visit to the University of Padua.

Founded in 1222, the university is one of Italy's premier academic institutions, counting Casanova among its student body and Galileo Galilei among its faculty. Today, the school attracts students from across Italy and beyond.

I, in fact, spent my first year in Italy as an exchange student in Padua, attending liberal arts classes and absorbing Italian culture. This meant gathering together with fellow students and new friends around sunset in one of the city's three central squares—Piazza del Signore, Piazza delle Erbe, and Piazza della Frutta—and trying to blend in with the locals by sipping on spritzes as if our academic careers depended on it.

Made with wine, soda water, and a bitter liqueur, a spritz is a light and bubbly cocktail. It can be easily enjoyed on an empty stomach, making it an ideal aperitivo. When paired with a little Italian tea sandwich, or tramezzino, and lively conversation, a single spritz can quickly evolve into two or three, which is sort of the idea.

SPRITZ

First-time visitors to Padua are often taken aback by the color of the beverages consumed in every café they pass.

Vibrant red Campari and neon orange Aperol, two potable bitter liqueurs, are the building blocks of the city's aperitivo of choice: the spritz. Made with white wine, a bitter, and a splash of soda water, the spritz is indisputably the most popular aperitivo, not only in Padua, but in the Veneto region as a whole.

The spritz is not entirely of Italian engineering. It's believed that during the Hapsburg occupation of northeastern Italy, Austrian soldiers, unaccustomed to the strong wines of the area, would add a *spritzen* of water to their wine. To this day if you order a spritz in Trieste, it will be served the way the Austrians would have drunk it, *bianco,* without the addition of a colorful bitter liqueur.

This is just one among the endless variations on the spritz. Following are a few recipes to get you started, but feel free to experiment with the ingredients, their doses, and garnishes.

The Basics

The basic spritz recipe calls for three parts wine, still or sparkling, two parts bitter liqueur, and one part soda. Use these proportions as your guideline, but they are simply suggestions. The goal is to find a balance between the bitter and sweet elements.

Use a dry, light white wine, ideally something from the Veneto region like Soave, pinot bianco, or garganega. Prosecco is also a widespread alternative.

Next comes the bitter element. Italy is home to a variety of potable bitters. Compared to cocktail bitters, which are highly concentrated both in alcohol and flavor and added to cocktails by the dash, these drinkable bitter liqueurs are meant to be sipped on their own or mixed into drinks by the ounce. Potable bitters can be further divided into two categories: those intended to be drunk before dinner, aperitivo bitters, and those for after a meal, *digestivo* (or digestive) bitters. In Italy, aperitivo bitters can usually be identified by their bright colors and often carry the label bitter rosso. Two noted exceptions include Rabarbaro Zucca (see page 51) and Cynar, a brown, artichoke-based bitter.

Dark and viscous, digestivo bitters are known as *amaro* (singular) and *amari* (plural), the Italian word for "bitter." They can range from the bracingly bitter, like Fernet-Branca, to the more balanced varieties, like Averna and Ramazzotti. Amari are generally drunk neat or served with a cube of ice.

When it comes to preparing a spritz, aperitivo bitters are preferred. Add a splash of Cynar to your next Campari spritz or seek out lesser-known brands the next time you are in Italy. The famed grappa house Nardini makes a variety of bitters, labeled *rosso*, *rabarbaro*, and *mezzoemezzo*. Some smaller-batch alternatives are available in the United States, like Cappelletti (similar to Campari) and Luxardo Aperitivo (similar to Aperol). Look for them online or in specialty wine and spirit stores.

And last but not least, the soda water. A spritz should sparkle from start to finish and my feeling is the more bubbles, the merrier. Sparkling mineral water, which is less carbonated than soda water, tends to go flat quickly. If you plan to use sparkling water, be sure to purchase it in small bottles or carbonate it at home in small quantities.

CAMPARI SPRITZ

1½ ounces dry white wine
1 ounce Campari (see page 71)
½ ounce soda water
1 orange slice
1 large green olive, optional

Fill a rocks glass with 3 or 4 ice cubes. Add the white wine, Campari, and soda water. Stir with a bar spoon, then add the orange slice and an olive on a coctail skewer.

Variations

APEROL SPRITZ
Substitute Aperol (see page 131) for Campari and proceed as described above.

SPRITZ AL SELECT
Substitute Select (see page 131) for Campari and garnish with a slice of lemon.

SPRITZ BIANCO
Fill a rocks glass with 3 or 4 ice cubes and add equal parts still white wine and soda water. Stir and finish with a slice of lemon and no olive.

HUGO SPRITZ
Fill a rocks glass with 3 or 4 ice cubes. Add 2 ounces Prosecco, 2 ounces soda water, and 1 ounce elderflower syrup (see page 131). Stir and garnish with a couple of fresh mint leaves.

Aperol

> Less antiseptic than Campari, both in terms of flavor and alcohol content (11% versus 28%), Aperol is a neon orange bitter liqueur made according to a recipe patented by the Barbieri family of Padua in 1919. The recipe calls for a proprietary blend of aromatics that includes bitter orange peel, Chinese rhubarb, and gentian. Its lightness and cheerful color make it perfect for summer cocktails.

Select

> Venetians distance themselves from more commercial bitters like Campari or Aperol by ordering their spritzes with Select. Created in 1920 on the island of Murano and little known outside the Veneto, Select is slightly sweeter than Campari and deeper in color. In Venice, a spritz with Select is always garnished with a slice of lemon, once again to set it apart from those made with Campari or Aperol, but also as a symbolic reference to the original spritz, the spritz *bianco,* made with lemon and without the addition of bitters.

Elderflower Syrup

> For generations, Italians living in the Dolomites have collected forest flowers and berries, using them to infuse syrups and distillates. Following the wave of popularity of the spritz in other parts of northeastern Italy, a bartender in the mountain town of Bolzano decided to create an alpine version of the spritz using elderflower syrup. The Hugo, as it was inexplicably named, has since made its way down the mountain and is served in most bars in Venice, Padua, and Treviso. When preparing a Hugo spritz at home, you can either make your own elderflower syrup or purchase the premade stuff at Ikea or online from the French company Monin, which specializes in flavored syrups. St.-Germain elderflower liqueur can also be used, but you may want to reduce the amount of Prosecco to account for the added alcohol.

Although I am lacking hard evidence, the vast majority of the times I have been served an aperitivo cocktail in Italy, it was accompanied by a bowl of potato chips. Shocking, right? Italians can't seem to get enough of fried sliced potatoes. Recently in Padua, however, many bars have begun serving pane carasau, *the traditional flatbread of Sardinia, in place of potato chips. Commonly referred to as* carta da musica, *or sheet music, this paper-thin, crispy bread literally crackles in your mouth. I suggest buying it in bulk at a specialty food store or Italian deli (whole sheets measure over a foot in diameter so they are often sold cut in half or in quarters) as it can be stored for up to a couple of months and is simple to serve. Drizzled with good olive oil (to create* pane guttiàu*) and toasted in the oven, the bread begins to really sing. Add a little flaky sea salt and some herbs, and you have an aperitivo worthy of a party. My favorites are dried oregano flowers or pounded fennel seeds, but dried rosemary or marjoram work as well. Serve with everything.*

PANE CARASAU
WITH OLIVE OIL AND HERBS

◦{ Makes **6** to **8** aperitivo servings }◦

6 sheets pane carasau (Sardinian flatbread), halved or quartered

Extra virgin olive oil

Flaky sea salt, such as Maldon

Dried oregano or fennel seeds

Preheat the oven to 250°F. Arrange the pane carasau in a single layer on two baking sheets. Drizzle with the olive oil and sprinkle sparingly with the salt and herbs. Toast in the oven for about 5 minutes. The bread should be crisp, but not browned. Stack on a plate and serve.

Note If you are interested in taking on the challenge of making pane carasau at home, Marcella Hazan's instructions found in her book *Marcella Cucina* achieve the most authentic results I have found in English, or Italian, for that matter.

Padua is home to a heritage chicken called the gallina padovana *or Paduan hen, which can be easily identified in a line-up by the tuft of long feathers sprouting from its head, not unlike the headpiece of a Vegas showgirl. Its dark meat was traditionally cooked for hours in a pig's bladder as part of a preparation called* alla canevera. *This recipe calls for simple poached chicken breasts (without the pig's bladder), which are marinated overnight with a mixture of herbs and balsamic vinegar to give the meat a pungent sweetness. If possible use traditional balsamic vinegar, or* aceto balsamico tradizionale di Modena, *which is darker and thicker than what is commonly sold as balsamic, having been made from reduced grape must and aged in wood barrels for a minimum of 12 years. The marinated chicken is then tossed with radicchio for color and a bitter note. Serve with a Morlacco and Tonic (page 153).*

RADICCHIO CHICKEN SALAD

⊹{ **Makes 6 to 8 aperitivo servings** }⊹

2 bone-in poached chicken breasts

¼ cup extra virgin olive oil, plus more for drizzling

Juice of ½ lemon

1 tablespoon traditional balsamic vinegar, plus more for drizzling (see headnote)

1½ tablespoons assorted chopped fresh herbs, such as a combination of basil, marjoram, thyme, parsley, and/or dill

Fine sea salt and freshly ground black pepper

1½ cups sliced radicchio (about ½ medium head)

Pull apart or slice the poached chicken into small pieces. Place the meat in a glass bowl or ceramic dish. Add the olive oil, lemon juice, balsamic vinegar, and chopped herbs. Season with fine sea salt and pepper and toss together well. Cover with plastic wrap and refrigerate the chicken overnight, or at least 2 hours ahead, to let the flavors develop.

Allow the chicken to come to room temperature, then toss with the radicchio. Divide the salad among small bowls and finish each with a drizzle of olive oil and balsamic vinegar.

Broccoli rabe, or cime di rapa, *has a somewhat bitter, but intensely green flavor that pairs nicely with a little spice and ricotta salata, a sheep's milk cheese that has been salted, pressed, and aged for a couple months. Serve with a bright white wine, like a Pinot Grigio, or a red with minimal tannins, like a Barbera.*

BROCCOLI RABE AND RICOTTA SALATA CROSTINI

⋅{ **Makes 6 to 8 aperitivo servings** }⋅

All'Ombra della Piazza

¼ cup extra-virgin olive oil

2 large garlic cloves, thinly sliced

¼ teaspoon crushed red pepper flakes

1 pound broccoli rabe, blanched until tender

1 teaspoon fine sea salt

Squeeze of fresh lemon juice

20 crostini (see recipe page 185)

4 ounces ricotta salata

20 oven-roasted grape tomatoes, optional (see recipe page 152)

Zest of one lemon, optional

Heat the olive oil, garlic, and red pepper flakes in a large skillet over medium heat. As soon as the garlic begins to sizzle, add the broccoli rabe and toss to coat with the oil. Sauté for 3 minutes, then remove from the heat. Toss with the salt and squeeze of lemon juice. Transfer to a food processor and puree until fairly smooth. Transfer to a bowl and let cool to room temperature.

(The puree can be prepared a couple days ahead, stored in an airtight container in the fridge. Bring to room temperature before serving.)

Top each crostino with a tablespooon of broccoli rabe puree. Grate ricotta salata on top. If desired, finish each crostino with a roasted grape tomato or lemon zest.

Michele Birtig, a gifted Padua-based bartender, conjured up this recipe after returning from a trip to Mexico. A twist on the Margarita, this cross-cultural cocktail blends agave-based mezcal, lime juice, and Sangue Morlacco, sour cherry brandy produced just outside of Padua (see page 153). And to up your garnish game, follow Birtig's lead and try your hand at dehydrating sliced citrus.

SANGUE *Gran Caffè Diemme*

1 lime plus 1 ounce fresh lime juice

1 teaspoon fine sea salt

1½ ounces mezcal

½ ounce Luxardo Sangue Morlacco or cherry brandy

½ ounce curaçao or Grand Marnier

3 dashes grapefruit or orange bitters

1 dehydrated, or fresh, lemon slice, for garnish

Grate the zest of half the lime onto a small plate and mix with the salt. Cut a twist from the unzested lime half and set aside. Moisten the rim of a rocks glass with a wedge of lime. Dip the rim into the lime salt, shaking off any excess. Fill the glass with 3 or 4 ice cubes.

Combine the mezcal, Sangue Morlacco, curaçao, lime juice, and bitters in a shaker. Shake vigorously, then strain into the prepared glass. Garnish with the slice of lemon and a lime peel.

Perched in the Euganean Hills southwest of Padua, Al Sasso restaurant welcomes its guests at every meal with a small plate of fried battered sage leaves. Crispy and fragrant, the leaves are a true delight, especially when paired with a light white wine or a glass of Prosecco. The key is to serve them hot, which requires frying them in batches as your guests arrive.

FRIED SAGE LEAVES

Al Sasso

◦{ **Makes 6 to 8 aperitivo servings** }◦

1 bunch fresh sage leaves (about 60 leaves)

⅓ cup all-purpose flour, plus more if needed

Oil for frying

Fine sea salt

Pinch the sage leaves off their stems, then wash and pat them dry with paper towels. To make the batter, put ½ cup water in a soup bowl and gradually sift the flour into the water, stirring it with a fork until mixed. The batter should have the consistency of heavy cream; add a little more flour or water, as necessary.

Heat at least ½ inch of oil in a shallow heavy-bottomed pan over high heat. When the oil is hot enough (see instructions page 83), place a few leaves in the batter to coat. Use a fork to remove the leaves one at a time, sliding each one into the hot oil.

Working in batches to avoid overcrowding, fry the leaves until golden, about 1 minute per side. Using a slotted spoon, transfer them to a plate lined with paper towels. Sprinkle with salt and serve hot.

All'Ombra della Piazza is a wine bar with a natural slant located in the shadow, or ombra, of one of Padua's three main piazzas. Every evening, the glass counter in the front of the bar is filled with rows of crostini and polpette, *deep-fried croquettes of varying shapes and fillings, from round meatballs to flattened fish patties. Prepared daily by two women from Campania, these eggplant* polpette *have a slight kick, thanks to the addition of a little chili powder. If you are not one for spice, simply leave it out.*

EGGPLANT POLPETTE

All'Ombra della Piazza

⊹{ **Makes 4 to 6 aperitivo servings** }⊹

1 pound eggplant, unpeeled and cut into 1-inch cubes

¼ cup freshly grated Parmigiano Reggiano

2 tablespoons finely chopped fresh flat-leaf parsley

2 large eggs, beaten

½ teaspoon chili powder, or a pinch of cayenne pepper

3 tablespoons plus 1 cup fine dried breadcrumbs

Fine sea salt and freshly ground black pepper

Oil for greasing and frying

Preheat the oven to 350°F and grease a baking sheet. Place the cubed eggplant on the prepared baking sheet and bake until tender, about 30 minutes. Transfer the eggplant to a large plate or serving dish lined with paper towels. Cover with another layer of paper towels and press to release excess moisture. Reduce the oven temperature to 200°F. Coarsely chop the eggplant and transfer to a large bowl. Add the grated cheese, chopped parsley,

2 tablespoons of the beaten egg, the chili powder, and 3 tablespoons of the breadcrumbs. Season with salt and pepper. Mix thoroughly, mashing the eggplant with a fork.

Shape the eggplant mixture into twelve 2-inch-long croquettes. Place the remaining beaten egg in a shallow bowl. Put the remaining 1 cup breadcrumbs in a separate shallow bowl.

Working with one croquette at a time, dip each croquette into the egg, turning to coat and shaking off the excess. Next, dip the croquette in the breadcrumbs, pressing gently to adhere the crumbs and shaking off the excess.

Pour enough oil into a medium heavy-bottomed pan to reach at least 1 inch up the sides of the pan and set over high heat. When the oil is hot enough

(see instructions page 83) work in batches, adding the eggplant croquettes to the pan without crowding them. Cook until golden brown, turning once, about 2 minutes per side. Using tongs or a slotted spoon, transfer the croquettes to a rack set over a baking sheet to drain, then transfer the baking sheet to the warm oven while you prepare the remaining batches. Polpette are best served warm.

TRAMEZZINI AND FRANCOBOLLI

Tramezzini are tea sandwiches with an Italian accent: soft, crustless white bread filled with paper-thin prosciutto and oil-packed artichokes rather than cucumber and watercress. But unlike British tea sandwiches, tramezzini are generally washed down with a glass of wine or a spritz cocktail (page 127) in place of a pot of Earl Grey.

What may come as a surprise is just how popular tramezzini are in northern Italy. Throughout the Veneto region, you can find tramezzini everywhere; from Harry's Bar, where they are made fresh to order, to hundreds of cafés, supermarkets, and automated vending machines in train stations.

In most Italian cafés, tramezzini are prepared each morning and artfully layered on trays to expose their filling.

In Venice, you will also find mini tramezzini, which go by the name of *francobolli*, or "postage stamps." These bite-size sandwiches are perfect for parties—an open invitation for sampling more than one.

The term *tramezzino* (the singular form of tramezzini) was coined to replace the English word *sandwich* during the Fascist era when Mussolini banned any attempt at using non-Italian words. Gabriele D'Annunzio, famed Italian writer and poet, is believed to have originated the term, which can be translated as "a little something in between."

Traditionally, tramezzini are made with two slices of white bread, spread with mayonnaise, and stuffed with a little something, generally a simple combination of two or three ingredients. In Italy, you will find both triangular and rectangular tramezzini. Keep in mind that triangle sandwiches almost always have a bulge in the center. To re-create the authentic Italian shape, pile the filling high in the center and less so around the edges. Tramezzini are best prepared up to an hour before serving, otherwise the soft bread tends to get soggy from the mayonnaise. If you are tight on time, prep the sandwich fillings ahead and assemble the tramezzini just before your guests arrive.

TRAMEZZINI: VARIATIONS ON A THEME

Here are few of the most common tramezzini combinations you will find in cafés in northern Italy.

Name	*Start with . . .*	*Then add . . .*	*Notes*
Pomodoro e mozzarella	Sliced vine-ripened tomatoes	Sliced mozzarella	And possibly a basil leaf or two.
Verdure e ricotta	Sliced grilled vegetables (zucchini, eggplant, peppers)	Fresh, soft ricotta	Spread ricotta on a slice of bread and pile high with vegetables.
Tonno e uova	Oil-packed canned tuna	Sliced hard-boiled eggs	
Tonno e cipolle	Oil-packed canned tuna	Pickled cocktail onions	Mix tuna with a little mayonnaise, a drizzle of olive oil, and a squeeze of lemon.
Tonno e olive	Oil-packed canned tuna	Green or black olives, pitted and sliced	See above.
Gamberetti	Tiny boiled shrimp	Sliced lemon	
Cotto e uova	Thinly sliced prosciutto cotto	Sliced hard-boiled eggs	
Cotto e carciofini	Thinly sliced prosciutto cotto	Sliced oil-packed artichokes	In a pinch you can use canned artichoke hearts. Rinse well and drizzle with good extra virgin olive oil.
Cotto e funghi	Thinly sliced prosciutto cotto	Sliced, cooked button mushrooms	In most bars, the mushrooms come from a can, but if you were to make this at home try sautéing sliced fresh mushrooms in olive oil.
Porchetta e radicchio	Sliced slow-roasted pork	Sliced radicchio	
Porchetta e pepperoni	Sliced slow-roasted pork	Juicy grilled bell peppers	Possibly spread with a little mustard.
Sorpressa, fontina e cavolo cappuccio	Thinly sliced cured pork sausage from the Veneto	Fontina cheese and shredded raw cabbage	Other mild cured pork sausages can be substituted.

Tramezzino Bread

✂ Growing up in Southern California prior to the arrival of artisanal bakeries, let alone a Whole Foods or Trader Joe's, I was taught that bread was white and used for making grilled cheese or peanut butter and jelly sandwiches. It came presliced in a plastic bag, which sat in the refrigerator for weeks if not months without going bad. In our house, Pepperidge Farm was the brand of choice, but I will never forget the yellow, red, and blue dots decorating the bags of Wonder Bread served to me in neighbors' homes.

Once I discovered the joys of fresh, naturally leavened bread, I was convinced that there was no turning back, even if it cost me a significant portion of my monthly paycheck. All the white sandwich bread I had eaten up until then paled in comparison. I deemed it tasteless and soulless.

You can imagine my surprise, and even a little disappointment, to find crustless, white sandwich bread in cafés across northern Italy. How could it possibly appeal to cultured Italian palates?

It took me a couple of months to get over my culinary culture shock, but I gradually learned to appreciate the subtle pleasure of soft bread paired with a soft filling.

In more upscale and ingredient-driven establishments in Italy, sandwich bread (also known as Pullman loaf or *pain de mie*) is baked daily. The loaf is then sliced and the crusts are carefully cut off.

However, the majority of cafés and bars use inexpensive, store-bought sandwich bread with the crusts already removed. In wholesale markets, it is even sold in 2-foot-long rectangular slices, ready to be spread with mayonnaise, layered with fillings, and cut into a tray's worth of tramezzini.

Upon further investigation, I was relieved to find that even the supermarket sandwich bread in Italy is made with just a few ingredients, all of them pronounceable: durum wheat flour, water, olive oil, natural yeast, and sea salt. No additives or preservatives.

When making tramezzini at home, I suggest using fresh white sandwich bread with a tight crumb that will slice easily. If fresh bread is not an option, head to the supermarket and start reading labels. Look for breads without added sugar, often in the form of high-fructose corn syrup. Or simply succumb to the temptation of Pepperidge Farm or Wonder Bread and claim it's for old times' sake.

At Gran Caffè Diemme, located in Piazza dei Signori, the heart of Padua's lively aperitivo scene, soft white sandwich bread is filled with morsels of shrimp, then layered with colorful sliced vegetables (pictured on top, page 148). While shrimp is a more common tramezzino filling, boiled lobster meat would make for an appetizing alternative.

SHRIMP AND VEGETABLE TRAMEZZINI

Gran Caffè Diemme

{ **Makes 4 tramezzini (half sandwiches)** }

1 carrot, peeled and trimmed

1 zucchini, trimmed

1 stalk celery, trimmed

½ fennel bulb, trimmed and fronds removed

1½ tablespoons extra virgin olive oil

8 ounces cooked shrimp

3 tablespoons mayonnaise, Italian-style (see page 200) or store-bought

Fine sea salt and freshly ground black pepper

4 slices soft white sandwich bread

Use a box grater to grate the vegetables into slivers. Alternatively, julienne the vegetables.

Fill a medium saucepan with water, add a generous pinch of salt, and bring to a simmer. Fill a bowl with ice water. Blanch the vegetable slivers for a minute, just until slightly tender but still crisp to the bite, then drain and transfer the vegetables to the ice water to stop the cooking. Drain again and pat dry with kitchen towels.

In a bowl, toss the vegetables with the olive oil and season with salt and pepper. In a separate bowl, mix the shrimp with 2 tablespoons of the mayonnaise.

Arrange the bread slices on a cutting board or flat work surface. Spread some of the remaining mayonnaise atop each slice. Divide the shrimp mixture between two slices, layer vegetables on top, folding them if necessary. Then close the sandwiches with the remaining bread, mayonnaise-side down. To make four tramezzini, cut each sandwich in half either lengthwise or diagonally.

The patriotic combination of red bresaola, green arugula, and white Parmesan—the colors of the Italian flag—usually comes together in the form of a summer salad or pizza topping, but it also makes for an excellent tramezzino.

BRESAOLA, ARUGULA, AND GRANA TRAMEZZINI

›{ **Makes 4 tramezzini (half sandwiches)** }‹

2 tablespoons mayonnaise, Italian-style (see page 200) or store-bought

1 teaspoon olive oil

Zest of 1 lemon

4 slices white sandwich bread, crusts removed

4 ounces bresaola (air-dried salted beef)

½ cup loosely packed arugula, coarsely chopped

1 ounce Parmigiano Reggiano, thinly sliced

Freshly ground black pepper

In a small bowl, whisk together the mayonnaise, olive oil, and lemon zest.

Arrange the bread slices on a cutting board or flat work surface. Spread some of the mayonnaise atop each slice. Divide the bresaola between two slices, draping it back and forth to create small folds rather than laying it flat across the bread. Divide the arugula between the two remaining slices of bread and top with the sliced Parmigiano Reggiano. Season with pepper, then close the sandwiches, turning the bresaola onto the arugula. Cut both sandwiches in half on the diagonal to make four tramezzini.

These small Italian egg salad sandwiches (pictured on bottom, page 148) are truly a crowd-pleaser. Carbonara, the classic combination of bacon, eggs, and cheese, is traditionally served as a pasta sauce in and around Rome. Turns out it also makes for an irresistible tramezzino.

CARBONARA TRAMEZZINI
Gran Caffè Diemme

◦{ Makes **4** tramezzini (half sandwiches) }◦

4 ounces guanciale, pancetta, or good dry-cured bacon, cut into ¼-inch cubes

4 hard-cooked eggs (see Half Eggs recipe, page 176, for instructions), shelled and chopped

½ cup loosely packed grated Pecorino Romano

3 tablespoons mayonnaise, Italian-style (see page 200) or store-bought

Freshly ground black pepper

4 slices white sandwich bread, crusts removed

Heat a skillet or sauté pan over medium-high heat. Once hot, brown the guanciale until crispy and golden, about 2 minutes, tossing occasionally for even browning. Transfer the guanciale to a plate lined with paper towels and let cool.

In a bowl, mix together the guanciale, eggs, grated Pecorino Romano, 2 tablespoons of the mayonnaise, and a couple grindings of pepper.

Arrange the bread slices on a cutting board or flat work surface. Spread the remaining mayonnaise atop each slice. Divide the egg mixture between two slices, then close the sandwiches with the remaining bread, mayonnaise-side down. Cut both sandwiches in half either lengthwise or on the diagonal to make four tramezzini.

FRITTATAS

Frittatas are a perfect aperitivo food. They are easy to prepare and require just a few staple ingredients. Plus, they can be made up to a day or two in advance, stored in the fridge, and served at room temperature, making for one less thing to think about on the day of your aperitivo party.

Italians will add practically anything to a frittata, from leftover pasta to a handful of wild herbs. Here are a few of my favorite recipes to get you started, but feel free to play around with what's in your vegetable garden or pantry.

BASIC EGG FRITTATA

⊹{ Makes **6** to **8** aperitivo servings }⊹

4 large eggs

¼ cup freshly grated Parmigiano Reggiano

½ teaspoon fine sea salt

Freshly ground black pepper

1 teaspoon extra virgin olive oil

In a medium bowl, gently whisk the eggs, grated Parmigiano Reggiano, salt, and a couple grindings of pepper.

In an 8-inch nonstick pan or cast-iron skillet, heat the olive oil over medium heat. Pour in the egg mixture and as it begins to set, use a spatula to lift the cooked egg away from the rim toward the center, allowing raw egg to run to the edges. Cook the frittata until fully set, about 5 minutes, then reduce the heat to low and continue cooking for 2 minutes.

Begin loosening the frittata from the pan by running a spatula around the edges. Shake the pan: the frittata should move as a whole. If it's still runny, cover the frittata and let it stand for 3 minutes. If it sticks, carefully slip the spatula farther under the frittata to separate it from the bottom of the pan.

Cover the pan with a lid or a dinner plate and turn the frittata over. Slide the frittata back into the pan, uncooked-side down, and cook over medium heat until golden, about 3 minutes.

Run the spatula around the edge of the frittata again and flip it onto a plate. Allow the frittata to rest for at least 5 minutes, then cut it into 1½-inch squares. Serve at room temperature with a small jar of toothpicks.

Note When doubling the recipe, you can choose to prepare two smaller frittatas or make one large frittata in a 12-inch pan. Cooking times will vary, so rather than following time cues, use common kitchen sense to judge when the frittata is done. Practice makes perfect.

Variations

RADICCHIO AND SPECK FRITTATA

In an 8-inch nonstick or cast-iron pan, sauté ¼ cup chopped onion in 1 tablespoon extra-virgin olive oil over medium heat until translucent, about 2 minutes. Add ¼ cup diced speck and cook until it begins to brown, about 3 minutes. Add 2 cups sliced radicchio, increase the heat to high, and sauté, stirring often, until the radicchio has wilted and deepened in color, about 3 minutes. Remove from the heat and wipe the pan clean. Stir the radicchio mixture into the beaten eggs before returning the mixture to the pan, then proceed as described on page 151.

ASPARAGUS FRITTATA

Break or cut off ½ inch from the tips of a small bunch of asparagus and reserve. Cook the asparagus stalks in boiling salted water until just tender to the fork. Drain and cut into ¼-inch slices. Stir 1 cup of the sliced asparagus and the reserved asparagus tips into the beaten eggs. Pour the egg mixture into an 8-inch nonstick skillet or pan, then proceed as described on page 151.

OVEN-ROASTED TOMATO AND BASIL FRITTATA

Preheat oven to 450°F. Cut 1 cup cherry or grape tomatoes in half and toss with a tablespoon of extra virgin olive oil and a teaspoon of salt. Put tomatoes in a baking dish lined with parchment paper and roast them, uncovered, until the tomatoes soften and begin to blister, 12 to 15 minutes. Stir ½ cup chopped oven-roasted tomatoes and 2 tablespoons julienned fresh basil into the beaten eggs before pouring them into an 8-inch nonstick skillet or cast-iron pan, then proceed as described on page 151. Save extra roasted tomatoes for a second frittata or to top a crostino (see page 186).

Not unlike a spritz (see page 127), this sparkling aperitivo is a balancing act of flavors. But in this case, the roles have been reversed: the bitterness comes from the tonic water and the sweetness from a special cherry brandy called Sangue Morlacco. Made from sour marasca cherries grown by the Luxardo family in the Euganean Hills outside Padua, Sangue Morlacco is the infusion of fermented sour cherry juice—also used to make their better known maraschino liqueur—alcohol, and sugar. It has a vibrant purple-red color and a tart cherry and almond aroma.

MORLACCO AND TONIC

1 ounce Luxardo Sangue Morlacco or cherry brandy

2½ ounces good-quality tonic water (see page 107)

Orange peel

Brandied cherry, optional

Fill a rocks glass or white wine glass with 3 or 4 ice cubes. Add the Sangue Morlacco and top with the tonic. Stir and serve with the orange peel and brandied cherry, if desired.

This is a great recipe to serve when there is a bit of a nip in the air or when it's downright freezing outside. The rich, creamy Gorgonzola slowly melts into the warm celery root puree, making for a simple yet satisfying combination. The celery root puree can be prepared up to three days ahead of time and reheated before serving. Potato puree or a mixture of celery root and potato are both worthy substitutes.

CELERY ROOT AND GORGONZOLA CROSTINI *All'Ombra della Piazza*

◦{ Makes **6** to **8** aperitivo servings }◦

12 ounces peeled celery root (about 1 medium), cut into 1-inch pieces

¼ cup milk

3 tablespoons unsalted butter, melted

Fine sea salt and freshly ground black pepper

20 crostini (see recipe page 185)

7 ounces Gorgonzola dolce

Leaves from 1 small bunch of celery or parsley, chopped

Put the celery root in a medium saucepan and add enough water to cover. Bring to a simmer over medium heat, then simmer until the celery root is tender, 20 to 30 minutes. Pass the celery root through a vegetable mill, or transfer it to a bowl and mash with a potato masher until it's fairly smooth. Stir in the milk and melted butter; season with salt and pepper.

Top each crostino with the celery root puree and a teaspoon of Gorgonzola. Finish with the chopped celery or parsley leaves and serve the crostini warm.

Freshly squeezed orange juice and seasoned tomato juice are standard when it comes to nonalcoholic aperitivi. Pink grapefruit, or pomplemo rosa, *is a refreshing alternative, especially when it's married with the delicate floral notes of chamomile and rose water.*

BOCCA DI ROSA

Caffè Tinto

1 tablespoon honey or agave nectar
1½ ounces hot chamomile tea
3 ounces fresh pink grapefruit juice
½ ounce fresh lime juice
2 drops rose water

Stir the honey into the chamomile tea until dissolved. In a cocktail shaker, combine the sweetened tea, grapefruit juice, lime juice, and rose water with 5 ice cubes. Shake vigorously, then strain into a glass of your choice.

ROME

In and around Rome, gnocchi are often made with semolina or coarsely ground durum wheat flour, rather than potato. Gnocchi alla romana are generally served as a primo piatto, *or the first course after an appetizer, but they can be easily presented in small bowls or ramekins as a warm and welcome aperitivo. I enjoy the aroma of sage and gladly garnish each portion with a leaf. Also try topping each portion with a tablespoon of leftover tomato or Amatriciana sauce.*

BAKED SEMOLINA GNOCCHI

∗{ **Makes 6 to 8 aperitivo servings** }∗

1 quart whole milk	4 tablespoons (½ stick) unsalted butter
2 teaspoons fine sea salt	1 cup freshly grated Parmigiano Reggiano
1 cup semolina	
2 egg yolks	16 fresh medium sage leaves

Pour the milk into a large saucepan and bring to a simmer over medium heat. Once bubbles form around the edge of the pan, reduce the heat to low. Add the salt, then, using your hands, slowly add the semolina, allowing the flour to gradually fall through your fingers, stirring continuously with a long-handled wooden spoon to prevent clumps from forming. Continue to cook and stir for 15 to 20 minutes or until the gnocchi mixture has come together and no longer sticks to the sides of the pan. Remove from the heat and stir in the egg yolks, 2 tablespoons of the butter, and ⅔ cup of the grated Parmigiano Reggiano.

Lightly grease a large baking sheet (18 by 13 inches) or an 8 by 12-inch sheet of aluminum foil. Pour the gnocchi batter out onto the prepared pan or foil and use a spatula to spread the batter into a ½-inch-thick rectangle. Let it cool on a flat surface.

Once the gnocchi batter has cooled completely and solidified, about 15 minutes, cut it into

continued —»

disks using a 2½-inch round ring mold, cookie cutter, or glass to create 32 disks in all. If the gnocchi sticks to the tool you are using, dip it in cold water.

Preheat the oven to 400°F. Arrange the round gnocchi on a greased baking sheet. Top each disk with a tiny knob of butter and half of the disks with a sage leaf. Dust all the gnocchi with the remaining ⅓ cup grated Parmigiano Reggiano. Bake on the uppermost rack of the oven for 15 minutes or until golden.

Remove the baking sheet from the oven and set out 16 oven-proof small bowls or ramekins. Using a metal spatula, carefully transfer two gnocchi into each bowl, stacking one with a sage leaf on top of one without. Serve the gnocchi warm. To reheat, place the small bowls on multiple baking sheets and heat under the broiler for 3 minutes.

Note Semolina gnocchi can be easily prepared up to 2 days in advance. Prepare the batter as directed and cut it into disks. Cover the disks in plastic wrap or sealed in a container and store in the fridge. When you're ready to serve the gnocchi, remove them from the refrigerator and follow the baking instructions above.

From the word bruscare, *meaning to toast, bruschetta* (brooh-SKEH-ta) *is basically toasted garlic bread. And, as with any seemingly simple Italian recipe, the secret is in the quality of the ingredients. Grape or cherry tomatoes are usually a good bet. As for the bread, look for a rustic or country-style loaf made from a natural starter—something around 8 by 12 inches is ideal—and good-quality extra virgin olive oil, is a must. The bread also can be arranged on a baking sheet and toasted for 5 to 7 minutes in a 425°F oven or grilled until brown and crisp.*

SUMMER TOMATO BRUSCHETTA

›{ Makes **6** to **8** aperitivo servings }‹

16 ounces fresh tomatoes

½ cup extra virgin olive oil, plus extra for drizzling

1 tablespoon flaky sea salt, such as Maldon, plus more for finishing

12 fresh basil leaves, hand torn, or 2 teaspoons dried oregano

6 slices rustic bread, cut in half

1 clove garlic

Freshly ground black pepper

Coarsely dice the tomatoes and put them in a medium bowl. Add the olive oil, salt, and basil or oregano. Toss to mix and set aside. Toast the bread in a toaster until the edges turn dark brown and the centers are golden. Arrange the toast on a serving plate. Slice off the tip of the garlic clove and rub the exposed end across each piece of toast. Drizzle a little olive oil across each slice, then top each with ⅓ cup of the tomato mixture. Finish with a tiny pinch of salt and a grinding of pepper.

Variation

WINTER TOMATO BRUSCHETTA

If the tomatoes you find aren't ripe and sweet, pass on the fresh ones and grab a can of the very best peeled Italian tomatoes. Substitute 2 cups peeled tomatoes, drained of their sauce, for fresh tomatoes. Add 2 tablespoons rinsed salt-packed capers to the other bruschetta toppings and proceed as described above.

ITALIAN CRAFT BEER

Beer certainly isn't the first thing that comes to mind when daydreaming of Italy. Even with the arrival of Peroni in 1846 and Birra Moretti in 1859, beer was considered a cold, refreshing alternative to water. Many Italians still think of beer in this way, whereas wine is a far superior beverage, revered as the nectar of the gods and underpinning of society.

So it may come as quite a surprise that Italy has developed a dynamic craft beer culture over the past three decades. Beginning in the mid-nineties, a handful of pioneering artisan brewers set up shop in northwest Italy. Initially, two schools of brewing came into being based on geography and influence: beers produced in Piedmont tended to be Belgian in style, while the pilsners and lagers coming out of Lombardy resembled beers from Germany and the Czech Republic. More recently, a third brew hub has developed in central Italy, drawing upon a more American style of craft brewing with in-your-face hops and no-limits experimentation.

During this time, Rome has emerged as Italy's craft beer capital, thanks to the city's beer bars and beer-centric restaurants, known for sourcing the best Italy has to offer, putting it on display, and making it accessible to a wider audience. Take, for example, Open Baladin. In this Roman temple of craft beer you will find forty Italian labels on draft at all times and another hundred bottles lining the wall behind the bar. Named best beer bar in the world in 2010 by Rate Beer, the Oscars of the craft beer world, Ma Che Siete Venuti a Fà is another not-to-be-missed destination for craft beer lovers. Manuele Colona, owner of "Macche," as locals refer to the bar, knows more about craft beer than most brewers.

Thankfully, many of the beers on tap in Rome's top beer bars are now being imported to the United States. Eataly has the widest assortment, but Italian wine shops around the country are starting to carry a variety of labels as well. Ask a salesperson to help guide you through the selection.

Chapter 4

VENICE

Venice is an aperitivo wonderland. All you need to know is some basic Venetian vernacular to eat and drink like a local. The city's streets are dotted with wine bars, or *bacari,* serving tapas-like portions of traditional Venetian fare known as *cicchetti*, to be consumed with a small glass of wine or *ombra*. In the decades of the Republic of Venice, which dated from the late seventh through the end of the eighteenth century, Venice was a major trading port, and drinking an ombra in a bacaro was considered essential to deal making.

In contrast to wine bars in other Italian cities, Venetian bacari remain open all day, allowing you to eat and drink your way through the city from dawn to dusk. Serious food and wine lovers should consider spending a day doing just that. Start your morning with a visit to the Rialto market (pictured on pages 178 and 201) to catch up on your Adriatic fish nomenclature, then stop at All'Arco for *sarde in saor* (page 190), or marinated sardines, and a mid-morning Prosecco. Cross the Rialto Bridge to pay a visit to Al Portego for a more substantial sampling of Venetian classics, like cuttlefish in its ink with polenta. Spend the afternoon getting lost and working up an appetite for a mini anchovy pizza (page 207) at Aciugheta, followed by a martini cocktail (page 204) and a heavenly meatball (page 202) from Harry's Bar. Then wake up and do it all over again.

BELLINI

The Bellini—the classic combination of white peach puree and sparkling wine—was made famous by Giuseppe Cipriani of Harry's Bar back in the thirties. In Venice's better bars, it is still seasonal, served exclusively during the summer when white peaches are available. Nowadays you can find frozen white peach puree fairly easily and drink Bellinis year-round. However, the satisfaction of making white peach puree with a food mill and a fine-mesh sieve is not to be underestimated. Neither is sipping this cocktail from a chilled glass during the height of summer.

BELLINI

Temperature is key to a great Bellini: make sure your peach puree, Prosecco, and glasses are all well chilled.

3 ounces dry Prosecco, chilled

1 ounce cold white peach puree (fresh or frozen and defrosted)

Pour the Prosecco into a well-chilled Champagne flute. Add the peach puree and stir gently to blend.

Note When making Bellinis for a group, prepare a pitcher just as your guests begin to arrive. Mix 1 cup cold white peach puree with a chilled bottle of Prosecco.

Fresh White Peach Puree

⊰{ **Makes about 4 ounces** }⊱

1 pound ripe white peaches

1 teaspoon fresh lemon juice

Simple syrup (see page 51) as needed, up to 2 tablespoons

Peel and core the peaches, then cut them into chunks. Pass through a food mill and collect the peach pulp in a bowl. Transfer the pulp to a fine-mesh sieve and force the pulp through using the back of a spoon, pressing on the solids to release the juices. Stir in the lemon juice to prevent browning. If your peach puree is tart, sweeten it with simple syrup to taste. Cover and refrigerate for up to a day. Stir before using.

BELLINI: VARIATIONS ON A THEME

Let the seasons be your guide to serving one of these variations on the classic Bellini.

Simply mix 1 part fruit puree or juice with 3 parts Prosecco, or to make virgin cocktails, substitute sparkling apple cider for the Prosecco.

Name	Fruit puree or juice	Instructions
Rossini	Strawberry puree	Pass the strawberries through a food mill or puree them in a blender, then pass them through a fine-mesh sieve. If necessary, adjust the flavor with simple syrup, lemon juice, or both.
Donatello	Melon puree	Puree chunks of a yellow-fleshed melon (such as a Canary melon) in a blender.
Mimosa	Orange juice	Sadly, in the States, the Mimosa has been given a bad rap. Often served together with subpar Bloody Marys during all-you-can-drink brunch service, this tart aperitivo—properly made with 1 part freshly squeezed orange juice with a splash of fresh tangerine juice and 3 parts chilled Prosecco—was originally served only in the winter when citrus is at its best. Experiment with what's available at the market. Blood oranges make for beautiful Mimosas.
Tiziano	1 ounce Concord grape juice and 1 teaspoon strawberry puree	In Italy, the Tiziano is made with the juice of *uva fragola* (or the "strawberry grape"), a small, dark purple grape used in the Veneto to make a sweet, sparkling red wine called *fragolino*. The wine has been banned due to a lack of controlled production, so unless you grow *uva fragola* yourself, your best bet is to blend some strawberry puree into grape juice.
Puccini	Mandarin juice	Freshly squeeze mandarins or clementines. Ideal in the winter when citrus is at its sweetest.
Bonaparte	Blueberry juice	Puree blueberries in a blender, then pass them through a fine-mesh sieve. Or look for 100% blueberry juice at the store.

Prosecco versus Champagne

To set the record straight, Prosecco is not Italian Champagne. Sure, it sparkles, but it's an entirely different wine, made with different grapes, using a different technique. It's intended to be drunk young, and is fairly low in alcohol. Its flavor is decidedly less complex than that of Champagne and its price tag reflects these factors.

Named after a small town about six miles from Trieste, Prosecco is made primarily with glera, a white grape native to the Carso region, now grown throughout the Veneto and Friuli-Venezia Giulia. Nowadays the best Prosecco is believed to come from the Valdobbiadene and Conegliano appellations, both located outside Treviso, where the grapes' origin and the winemaking method are protected with the Italian Denominazione di Origine Controllata (DOCG) status.

Most Prosecco producers use the Charmat (or Martinotti) method, whereby the wine undergoes a secondary fermentation, which produces the sparkle, using large stainless-steel tanks and is then bottled under pressure. Champagne is made by a significantly more labor-intensive and expensive process known as *méthode champenoise*, or *metodo classico* in Italian, which calls for the wine to be bottle-fermented and aged on its lees (residual yeast). During aging, the bottles are placed in racks, top-down at a 45-degree angle, and rotated (or riddled), often by hand, so that the lees collect in the neck of the bottle. Then the lees are removed, a little sugar is added (or not), and a cork is inserted into the bottle and ultimately topped with a wire cage.

Italian sparkling wines most similar to those from Champagne are made in Franciacorta and Trentino, where they are made using chardonnay, pinot noir, and pinot meunier grapes according to the méthode champenoise.

Due in part to the return to making wine in a natural way—meaning, in short, without the use of pesticides in the vineyards or engineered strains of yeast in the cellar—a distinct style of Prosecco has re-emerged in recent decades. Known as *sur lie* or "on its lees" in French, the wine is bottle-fermented and aged with the yeasts, which are intended to give substance and balance. The Italian term for sur lie wines is *col fondo*, also written *Colfòndo*. The often-cloudy result is almost savory or salty. In the States, you can find Colfòndo Prosecco in most specialized Italian wine stores. It should be drunk on its own and is not recommended for preparing Bellinis and other Prosecco-based aperitivi.

Leave it to the Italians to do simple well, like pair boiled eggs and anchovies. This curious combination, known locally as mezzi ovi, *or "half eggs," has become a Venetian classic, a simpler and more stylish version of deviled eggs. For a more sophisticated* spuntino, *or snack, use quail eggs and a square of anchovy.*

HALF EGGS

⊰{ **Makes 6 to 8 aperitivo servings** }⊱

6 large eggs (see Note)
12 salt- or oil-packed anchovy fillets

Freshly ground black pepper

Put the eggs in a large pot and add enough water to cover by 1 inch. Bring to a simmer over high heat. As soon as the water forms tiny bubbles around the edge of the pot, remove from the heat and cover the pot. Let the eggs sit for about 8 minutes. Meanwhile, fill a large bowl with ice water.

Remove the eggs from the pot and transfer to the ice water to chill. To shell the eggs, crack each shell by tapping all over with the back of a spoon. Starting at the wide or bottom end, remove a piece of the shell and pull back the membrane, hopefully bringing the rest of the shell with it. (Eggs that are one or two weeks old are actually easier to shell.)

Halve each egg lengthwise. Rinse the anchovies well and pat dry with paper towels, then top the egg halves with the anchovies by inserting a toothpick at an angle through each anchovy and into the thickest part of the egg white. Finish with a grinding of pepper and serve.

Note It's always a good idea to cook a couple extra eggs so you can check for doneness before transferring all the eggs to the ice water.

You will find a version of this sandwich in almost every café in Venice. What varies is the presentation of the egg: halved, sliced, or chopped. Capers and anchovies, both optional, provide little bursts of flavor, making each bite slightly different from the next.

TUNA AND EGG TRAMEZZINI

⋄{ **Makes 4 tramezzini (half sandwiches)** }⋄

1 cup canned tuna in olive oil, drained (from about three 6-ounce cans)

¼ cup plus 2 tablespoons mayonnaise, Italian-style (see page 200) or store-bought

2 teaspoons extra virgin olive oil

1 teaspoon fresh lemon juice

1 tablespoon salt-packed capers, rinsed and chopped, optional

2 salt- or oil-packed anchovy fillets, rinsed and chopped, optional

Fine sea salt and freshly ground black pepper

4 slices white sandwich bread, crusts removed

2 hard-cooked eggs (see Half Eggs, page 176, for instructions), shelled and cut into ¼-inch slices

In a medium bowl, combine the tuna with ¼ cup of the mayonnaise, the olive oil, the lemon juice, and the chopped capers and anchovies, if using, and mix thoroughly. Season with salt and pepper to taste.

Arrange the bread slices on a cutting board or flat work surface. Spread the remaining 2 tablespoons mayonnaise across the slices. Arrange the egg slices atop the mayonnaise on two of the bread slices, dividing them evenly. Top the egg with the tuna salad, then close the sandwiches with the remaining bread slices, mayonnaise-side down.

To make 4 tramezzini, cut each square sandwich in half on the diagonal.

Walter Bolzonella, beloved barman of Hotel Cipriani's Gabbiano Bar, came up with this seasonal spritz, which is served poolside on warm summer evenings. Part of its appeal is undeniably the setting. Take your first sip with your eyes closed and imagine yourself living the life of luxury in Venice. The original recipe calls for a sprayable star anise essential oil, but rubbing your glass with a pod will give the spritz a refreshing note of the spice.

WATERMELON SPRITZ
Gabbiano Bar

1 whole star anise pod

¾ ounce Campari (see page 71)

1½ ounces fresh watermelon juice (from about ½ cup diced watermelon flesh)

3 ounces Prosecco

Small watermelon slice

Fennel fronds

Rub the rim and inside of a large red wine glass with the star anise, then fill the glass with 3 ice cubes. Add the Campari, watermelon juice, and Prosecco. Lightly trace the star anise around the edge of the glass, then add it to the spirits. Garnish with a thin triangular slice of watermelon and fennel fronds.

Note To make fresh watermelon juice, trim the rind from the watermelon and puree the chunks of watermelon flesh in a blender, then pass through a fine-mesh sieve.

Hotel Cipriani bartender Walter Bolzano has once again spruced up a common cocktail for his sophisticated clientele. His twist on the Hugo Spritz (page 128) is called Nina's Passion, named by Gabbiano Bar regular George Clooney in honor of his mom. For this cocktail, the bartender's choice of sparkling wine is Bellavista Brut Franciacorta, a dry Champagne-style sparkling wine produced in the northern Italian region of Lombardy. Any brand of dry or brut Franciacorta or Champagne will do. In a pinch, you can use Prosecco, just don't tell George.

NINA'S PASSION

Gabbiano Bar

2 ripe passion fruit, or 1 tablespoon frozen passion fruit puree

1 ounce St-Germain elderflower liqueur

4 ounces dry sparkling wine, such as Bellavista Brut Franciacorta

Edible flowers, like nasturtiums, to garnish

If using fresh passion fruit, cut the fruit in half. Scrape out the pulp and seeds and pass them through a food mill to separate out the seeds. Filter the puree through a fine-mesh sieve.

Fill a large red wine glass with 3 or 4 ice cubes. Add the passion fruit puree, elderflower liqueur, and sparkling wine. Stir with a bar spoon and garnish with edible flowers.

CROSTINI

Crostini are small pieces of toasted bread that are used to transport a wide array of toppings to your mouth. When prepared properly, they are truly irresistible and will quickly become your go-to aperitivo food. Although in the United States, the terms *bruschetta* and *crostini* are often used interchangeably, they are actually two different preparations. Bruschetta (page 162) or bruschette (plural) are thick slices of grilled bread that are rubbed with garlic and topped with coarsely chopped tomatoes or other rustic ingredients. They can be eaten by hand but are more gracefully consumed with a fork and knife. Crostini are decidedly smaller, toasted and not grilled, and more sophisticated.

While the toppings are the real stars of the show, the bread is the fundamental building block to a great *crostino*. I generally use a baguette, but have been known to grab a loaf of ciabatta in a pinch. Save your sandwich bread for tramezzini, as it is too tender and often too sweet to stand up to the succulent toppings.

When it comes to toppings, the sky's the limit. You can use everything from yesterday's mashed potatoes and a dab of Gorgonzola to other creative combinations based on what's available in your pantry. As a rule of thumb, calculate a tablespoon or two of topping per crostino.

BASIC CROSTINI

{ Makes about 40 crostini }

1 baguette
About 1 cup extra virgin olive oil

Preheat the oven to 425°F. Slice the baguette about ½ inch think. If the bread is too soft to slice, try covering it with plastic wrap and placing it in the freezer for about 20 minutes. Arrange the bread slices on a baking sheet and lightly brush the tops with olive oil. Bake until golden brown with slightly darker brown edges, about 5 minutes. Let cool on the baking sheet. The crostini will continue to crisp as they cool.

CROSTINI: VARIATIONS ON A THEME

Here are some common Venetian crostini toppings to get you started.

Start with . . .	Then add . . .	Garnish
Oven-roasted tomatoes (see page 152)	balsamic vinegar	fresh basil
Oil-packed canned tuna	Italian-style mayonnaise (page 200)	sliced raw leeks
Sea bass or swordfish crudo (pictured opposite, center)	blanched spring peas	fresh mint
Seared sea scallops	chopped tomatoes	fresh basil
Oil-preserved artichokes	pitted black olives	
Prosciutto crudo	sliced figs or fig jam	sliced toasted almonds
Thinly-sliced pancetta (pictured on page 184)	sliced raw mushrooms	chopped parsley
Oven-roasted eggplant slices (pictured top on page 184)	burrata	
Fava bean puree	pecorino cheese, crumbled	fresh mint
Broccoli rabe (page 135)	ricotta salata	lemon zest
Winter squash puree	Gorgonzola	balsamic vinegar
Gorgonzola (pictured left on page 81)	honey	walnuts
Asiago (page 188)	almonds	mushrooms

At La Cantina, a lively wine bar located along Strada Nuova, chef and co-owner Francesco Zorzetto prepares crostini to order using only the best seasonal ingredients available. There is never a printed list. You are merely asked how hungry you are and if you want your crostini hot or cold, and with fish, meat, or cheese. The rest is up to Zorzetto and his imagination. Some of his artful crostini include tiny sea scallops called canastrelli *with ripe, red tomatoes and basil or boiled mantis shrimp,* canocchie, *with freshly shucked spring peas. If you don't have access to fresh fish pulled straight from the Adriatic, try this simple yet satisfying combination. And if you can't find Asiago cheese, substitute a young Gruyère.*

ASIAGO AND MUSHROOM CROSTINI *La Cantina*

⋅{ Makes **6** to **8** aperitivo servings }⋅

¼ cup extra virgin olive oil
½ teaspoon finely chopped garlic
4 cups sliced button mushrooms
1 teaspoon fine sea salt

Freshly ground black pepper
20 crostini (see recipe page 185)
4 ounces Asiago cheese, thinly sliced
½ cup sliced almonds

Heat the olive oil and garlic in a large sauté pan over medium heat. Cook and stir the garlic until pale gold, then add the sliced mushrooms. Turn over the slices a couple of times, then reduce the heat to low and cover the pan. Cook, stirring occasionally, for 5 to 10 minutes, or until the mushrooms are very soft. Uncover, raise the heat to high, and boil off the excess water. Season with the salt and a few grindings of pepper.

Arrange the crostini on a baking sheet. Top each crostino with a generous tablespoon of the sautéed mushrooms and a slice of the cheese. Sprinkle each crostino with a teaspoon of the sliced almonds. Broil under high heat for 2 minutes or until the cheese begins to melt. Serve immediately.

Al Portego, a small bacaro *tucked away at the end of a narrow street between Rialto and Piazza San Marco, serves an endless array of cicchetti prepared daily and displayed in baking dishes stacked high in a glass case. Baccalà three ways, sardines in another two, cuttlefish stewed in its ink, meatballs in tomato sauce, and sausage-stuffed mushrooms sit next to steamed artichokes, roasted peppers, and this roasted Romanesco, a pale green cauliflower from northern Italy with tight, pointy florets. A nod to Venice's past as a primary port for spices headed to western and northern Europe, the curry brightens the dish while making it slightly exotic. Roasted cauliflower can be prepared up to three days ahead; warm before serving.*

ROASTED ROMANESCO WITH CURRY

Al Portego

⊰{ **Makes 6 to 8 aperitivo servings** }⊱

1 head Romanesco cauliflower or regular (white) cauliflower, cored and cut into florets

3 tablespoons extra virgin olive oil, plus extra for greasing

2 teaspoons curry powder

2 teaspoons red wine vinegar

½ teaspoon fine sea salt

Freshly ground black pepper

Preheat the oven to 450°F. Put the cauliflower florets in a large bowl. Add the olive oil, curry powder, vinegar, salt, and a couple grindings of pepper. Toss well to coat the cauliflower completely.

Transfer the cauliflower to a greased baking sheet. Roast, tossing from time to time, until the cauliflower is tender and the edges are slightly browned, about 20 minutes. Serve warm in small bowls.

The sweet and sour flavor of this preparation, known as agrodolce *in Italian, is a trademark of Venetian cuisine. Originally, Venetian sailors would preserve the fish they caught out at sea by marinating it in cooked onions doused in vinegar. Today the custom is kept alive on the eve of the Festa del Redentore, the third Saturday of July, when Venetians gather on boats of all kinds in St. Mark's basin to watch fireworks and eat sardines in saor. Luckily for us, they are served year-round in many of the city's bacari, including All'Arco, located near the Rialto fish market, where they debone and butterfly the sardines for forkless eating.*

This is a great dish for aperitivo parties because it can—and should—be made a day or two ahead of time. This recipe is intended for larger groups of 12 to 16 people, but you can either halve the recipe for smaller parties or serve leftovers as an appetizer later in the week. And if you don't know your way around a sardine, ask your fishmonger to clean and prep the little fish for you. In the absence of fresh sardines at your local fish market, try using smelt, small mackerel, or another oily fish with an assertive flavor. When using fillets rather than whole fish, cut them into 1-inch pieces before frying.

SARDE IN SAOR CROSTINI *All'Arco*

◦{ Makes **20** aperitivo servings }◦

½ cup extra virgin olive oil

4 cups thinly sliced white onions (about 4 large onions)

1 cup white wine vinegar

3 tablespoons raisins, soaked in warm water for 5 minutes and drained, optional

1 tablespoon pine nuts, optional

40 fresh sardines (about 1 pound), heads removed, deboned, and butterflied

Oil for frying

All-purpose flour

Fine sea salt and freshly ground black pepper

40 crostini (see recipe page 185)

In a large skillet, heat the olive oil over low heat. Add the onions and cook until tender and translucent, stirring occasionally, about 20 minutes. (You may need to add a tablespoon of water to keep the onions from browning.) Add the vinegar, raise the heat to high, and bring to a boil while stirring. Reduce the heat to low and simmer for 1 minute, then remove from the heat and add the raisins and pine nuts, if desired.

Rinse the cleaned deboned sardines in cold water and pat dry with paper towels.

Heat ½ inch of oil in a shallow heavy-bottomed pan over high heat. Dredge both sides of the fish in the flour. Slip 1 sardine into the oil when it is hot enough (see instructions page 83). Working in batches to avoid overcrowding, add the remaining sardines to the pan and fry until golden brown, about 1 minute per side. Using a slotted spoon, transfer the fried fish to an 8 by 12-inch glass baking dish, forming a single layer. Season the fish with a little salt and a couple grindings of pepper, then spread the onion mixture on top. (If using a smaller baking dish, you may need to make two layers of sardines and saor: place half the sardines on the bottom of the dish, season with salt and pepper, cover with half the onion mixture, and repeat.)

Cover the dish and refrigerate for at least 24 hours before serving. Refrigerated, the sardines will keep for up to a week and the pungent flavor of the vinegar will penetrate the fish over time. Remove from the fridge an hour before serving to bring to room temperature.

Place one sardine on each crostino and top with a spoonful of the onion mixture.

Variation

PUMPKIN IN SAOR

Steam or roast 1 pound pumpkin cut into 1-inch cubes. Place the cooked pumpkin in a baking dish, cover with the prepared onions, and let stand for at least an hour, or refrigerate overnight, before serving. Serve spooned onto crostini.

Italian restaurateur Raffaele Alajmo and his brother, chef Massimiliano of Le Calandre restaurant in Padua, created this fresh and simple take on the Bloody Mary for their Venice outpost Gran Caffè and Ristorante Quadri (pictured opposite and on pages 170 and 175), located in St. Mark's Square. The key to this cocktail is finding the sweetest tomatoes possible. At Quadri they use bright red Italian datterini, but good grape or cherry tomatoes will do the job.

BLOODY RAF

Gran Caffè Quadri

4 ounces sweet grape or cherry tomatoes
Fine sea salt and freshly ground black pepper

1 ounce vodka, chilled
Extra virgin olive oil, for drizzling

Puree the tomatoes in a blender on high speed to make a thick puree. Strain the puree through a fine-mesh sieve, pressing on the solids with the back of a spoon to release all the juice, to make about ⅓ cup strained tomato juice. Season with salt and pepper to taste. Cover the puree and chill in the refrigerator until cold, about 30 minutes.

Pour the chilled tomato juice into a shaker (without ice). Add the vodka and shake vigorously to mix. Pour into a small chilled martini glass and finish with a little drizzle of olive oil.

Note When hosting an aperitivo party at home, prepare a pitcher of fresh tomato puree before your guests arrive. The juice can be made up to a day or two ahead of time and stored, covered, in the fridge. Before serving, add an ounce of vodka for every ⅓ cup juice and stir well. Pour into small martini glasses and garnish each serving with a little drizzle of olive oil.

Working for a chef has its advantages, many of which come in the edible form. My first day on the job as communications director for the Alajmo family restaurant group, I was treated to Chef Massimiliano's creamy stockfish puree, locally known as baccalà mantecato, *sandwiched between small squares of fried polenta (pictured on page 195). I was hooked at first bite. However, re-creating these little sandwiches at home presents some challenges, like days of soaking the stockfish or dried cod and hours, or what seems like hours, of whipping or beating the fish into a rich emulsion. If you can find prewhipped baccalà mantecato, use it. If not, use white fish pâté from your closest Jewish deli.*

WHITE FISH PÂTÉ AND CRISPY POLENTA *Gran Caffè Quadri*

⋅{ **Makes 8 to 10 aperitivo servings** }⋅

1 tablespoon fine sea salt

3½ cups coarse-grained Italian yellow polenta (cornmeal), or instant polenta

1 cup olive oil for frying, plus more for greasing the pan

2¼ cups (16 ounces) fish pâté (stockfish, salt cod, or smoked whitefish)

In a large, heavy pot, bring 8 cups water to a boil over high heat. Add the salt and reduce the heat to medium-high. Gradually add the polenta in a slow, steady stream, stirring continuously with a long wooden spoon or whisk. Make sure the water continues to boil as you add the polenta.

Reduce the heat to medium-low and cook, stirring in one direction, round and round and from the bottom of the pot upward, until the polenta forms a mass that pulls away from the sides of the pan, 30 to 40 minutes for long-cook polenta and 3 to 4 minutes for instant.

Oil a large rimmed baking sheet. Pour the warm polenta out onto the prepared pan, spreading it evenly with a well-oiled rubber spatula to a ½-inch thickness. To perfectly flatten the polenta, oil the bottom of a separate baking sheet and place it on top of the polenta. Press down gently until flat. Allow the polenta to set at room temperature, about 30 minutes. (At this point, if you don't plan to serve the sandwiches the same day, you can cover the pan of polenta with plastic wrap and store in the refrigerator for up to 3 days before cutting the polenta into squares and frying.)

When set, cut the polenta in the pan into forty-eight 2-inch squares. If the polenta is too soft for pan-frying, cover it with plastic wrap and chill in the refrigerator until firm enough to fry, about 20 minutes.

To fry the polenta squares, heat 2 tablespoons of the olive oil in a shallow heavy-bottomed pan over medium-high heat. Working in batches, fry the polenta squares in the hot oil until golden, turning once, about 1 minute per side. Once golden

brown on both sides, transfer the polenta squares to a wire rack and allow to cool to room temperature. Add more oil as necessary.

If you prefer, you can grill, rather than pan-fry, the polenta squares. To do so, brush both sides of the polenta squares with olive oil and place under a preheated broiler until very lightly charred on both sides.

To assemble the sandwiches, place a generous spoonful of the smoked fish pâté in the center of a polenta square, forming a mound. (You also can use a pastry bag fitted with a wide tip to have more control over this process.) Top with another polenta square and secure each sandwich with a toothpick. Repeat with the remaining polenta squares, smoked fish, and toothpicks.

Serve the sandwiches at room temperature, or reheat them briefly in the microwave.

Located along the long promenade that connects St. Mark's Square and the Giardini della Biennale, home to biannual contemporary art and architecture exhibitions, Ristorante Wildner offers great people-watching, as well as some of the best fried sardines in the city. Sit on the outdoor patio and let Luca Fullin, the restaurant's charming manager, introduce you to a lesser-known wine from the Friula-Venezia Giulia region to be paired with a small plate of sardines with salsa ruggine *or rusty sauce.* It should go without saying that the fresher the sardines, the better. Ask your fishmonger to clean and butterfly them before you take them home. The sardines should also be as cold as possible, so refrigerate them until ready to fry.

FRIED SARDINES WITH SALSA RUGGINE
Ristorante Wildner

⁖{ **Makes 6 to 8 aperitivo servings** }⁖

1½ cups mayonnaise, Italian-style (see page 200) or store-bought

1½ teaspoons paprika

1 teaspoon Italian chili oil (see Note, page 200)

Oil for frying

2 large eggs

About 2 cups fine dried breadcrumbs

24 fresh sardines, deboned and butterflied, heads removed

Fine sea salt

In a small bowl, whisk together the mayonnaise, paprika, and chili oil until the mayonnaise develops a uniform "rusty" color. Cover and refrigerate until ready to use.

Heat 2 inches of oil in a medium heavy-bottomed pan over medium-high heat.

Meanwhile, in a wide shallow bowl, lightly beat the eggs. Place 1 cup of the breadcrumbs in another wide shallow bowl.

Dip a sardine into the egg; turn to coat and shake off the excess. Dip the sardine in the breadcrumbs, pressing to adhere. Shake off any excess. Transfer the sardine to

continued —»

a large plate and repeat with the remaining sardines, adding more breadcrumbs as needed.

When the oil is hot enough (see instructions page 83) work in batches, carefully frying 4 sardines at a time, adjusting the heat if necessary (the oil should not smoke) until golden brown, about 45 seconds per side. Using a slotted spoon, transfer the sardines to a plate lined with paper towels. Dust with salt and serve each batch immediately with individual bowls of the "rust" sauce, then continue frying.

Note If you can't find Italian chili oil (*olio di peperoncino*), you can make your own quickly by heating 1 tablespoon olive oil and a shake of crushed red pepper flakes in a small saucepan over low heat for 4 minutes. Remove from the heat, let cool, and strain out the flakes.

Italian-Style Mayonnaise

I don't believe I have ever eaten a tramezzino in Italy that wasn't slathered with mayo, either homemade or store-bought.

◦{ **Makes about 1½ cups** }◦

2 large egg yolks, preferably organic, at room temperature

1¼ cups neutral-tasting vegetable oil, such as sunflower seed or grapeseed

Juice of ½ lemon

Fine sea salt to taste

¼ cup extra virgin olive oil

In a medium bowl, whisk the egg yolks using a flexible metal whisk until frothy. (Alternatively, you can use a handheld electric or stand mixer.) Gradually add ½ cup of the vegetable oil, a tablespoon at a time, whisking continuously until the mixture has thickened. Whisk in the lemon juice and a pinch of salt. Gradually add the remaining ¾ cups vegetable oil and ¼ cup olive oil, whisking continuously. Season with salt to taste.

The mayonnaise will keep, covered and refrigerated, for about a week.

Note While homemade mayonnaise is truly worth the time and energy, you can quickly doll-up the store-bought stuff by whisking ¼ cup good-quality extra virgin olive oil and the juice of ½ lemon into 1½ cups store-bought mayonnaise.

*When you order an aperitivo at Venice's legendary Harry's Bar,
a small plate of polpettine, perfectly tender fried meat patties,
will magically appear from the kitchen. Although Cipriani's recipe is
a closely guarded secret, this one comes close. You can even make these
patties a day or two in advance and reheat them in the oven. Use
a 1½-inch ring mold to shape the polpettine. Since this recipe uses
relatively small quantities of ground meat, make it when you have extra
left over. You can use chicken, veal, or whatever you have on hand.
Serve with a Bellini or a martini cocktail.*

HARRY'S BAR POLPETTINE

Harry's Bar

◦{ **Makes 6 to 8 aperitivo servings** }◦

½ ounce dried porcini mushrooms	¼ cup whole milk
1½ tablespoons extra virgin olive oil	1 slice stale bread, crusts removed
½ clove garlic	¼ cup mashed potatoes
1 fresh rosemary sprig	2 large eggs, beaten
4 ounces ground chicken	¼ cup grated Parmigiano Reggiano
4 ounces ground veal	1 cup fine dried breadcrumbs
Fine sea salt and freshly ground black pepper	Oil for frying

Soak the dried mushrooms in enough water to cover for at least 15 minutes. Drain, chop, and set aside.

Meanwhile, in a medium skillet, heat the olive oil, garlic, and rosemary over medium heat. As soon as the oil is hot and the garlic is just beginning to brown, remove and discard the garlic and rosemary. Add the chicken and veal to the pan and cook, breaking up the meat with the back of a wooden spoon. Season with salt and pepper and continue cooking, stirring occasionally, until the meat is evenly browned. Remove from the heat and transfer the meat to a medium bowl to cool slightly.

Pour the milk into a wide shallow bowl and add the bread, flipping it after a couple of minutes. When the bread has soaked up most of the milk, transfer the bread to the bowl containing the browned meat.

Add the mashed potato, half of the beaten eggs, the grated Parmigiano Reggiano, and chopped mushrooms to the bowl with the meat. Transfer the mixture to a food processor and pulse until light and uniform. Season with salt and pepper.

On a work surface, place 1 tablespoon of the meat mixture in a 1½-inch-wide ring mold and press down lightly to create an even thickness. Lift up the mold, flip the meat over, and flatten ever so slightly to round the edges, creating a small patty. Set aside on a platter or baking sheet while you prepare the remaining patties.

Place the remaining beaten egg into a shallow bowl, add a tablespoon of water, and beat gently until uniform in color. Put the breadcrumbs in a separate shallow bowl.

Working with one patty at a time, dip each patty into the egg. Turn to coat and shake off the excess. Dip the patty in the breadcrumbs, pressing gently to adhere, and shake off the excess. Return the coated patty to the platter or baking sheet and repeat to make the remaining patties.

Pour enough oil into a medium skillet to reach at least 1 inch up the sides and heat over high heat. When the oil is hot enough (see instructions page 83) and working in batches, add 6 to 8 patties to the pan and cook until the patties are golden brown, turning once, about 2 minutes per side. Using tongs or a slotted spoon, transfer the patties to a wire rack set over a baking sheet to drain. Repeat with the remaining patties.

Serve hot or allow to cool to room temperature.

HARRY'S BAR MARTINIS AND OTHER BATCHED COCKTAILS

If you ask for a martini cocktail at Harry's Bar, surprisingly it will not be made to order. Unless you ask otherwise, your martini will be pulled from the freezer, pre-poured into a small frosted glass, and placed on the bar in front of you. Although serious cocktail drinkers may scoff at the idea, by mixing and bottling the bar's most commonly requested gin drinks in advance, the bartenders are able to serve clients quickly and consistently.

Premixed and bottled cocktails are also great for parties. Just be sure to select preparations using ingredients that don't have a tendency to separate, like the cocktails included here. You'll need a clean 750-milliliter bottle (the standard size of a wine bottle) to make and chill the batched cocktail described here.

Remember that an aperitivo is intended to entice you to eat, not knock you out. Two ounces may not seem like a lot, but this drink is almost straight gin. Sip slowly—and should your guests request another martini, be sure to serve it in a new glass pulled straight from the freezer.

MONTGOMERY

›{ **Makes 12 small cocktails** }‹

Ernest Hemingway, a Harry's Bar regular beginning in 1949, drank his martinis dry—very dry: 15 parts gin to 1 part dry vermouth. He named his martini after British general Bernard Montgomery who, Hemingway claimed, would go into battle only if his troops outnumbered the enemy 15 to 1. Today, the proportion used at Harry's Bar is 10 to 1.

2¾ cups dry gin
2 ounces dry vermouth

Using a funnel, pour the gin and vermouth directly into a clean 750-ml wine bottle. Seal with a cork or screw cap and gently rotate the bottle back and forth to mix. Chill in the freezer until very cold.

For each serving, pour 2 ounces of the cocktail into a small chilled martini glass or large shot glass.

DOGE

{ Makes 12 small cocktails }

A Harry's Bar classic of yesteryear.

- 2 cups dry gin
- 1 cup Carpano Antica Formula sweet vermouth

Using a funnel, pour the gin and sweet vermouth directly into a clean 750-ml wine bottle. Seal with a cork or screw cap and gently rotate the bottle back and forth to mix. Chill in the freezer until cold.

For each serving, pour 2 ounces into a small chilled martini glass.

NEGRONI

{ Makes 12 small cocktails }

Negroni purists will argue for adding a splash of water, representative of the ice that would melt and dilute your cocktail if made to order with room temperature ingredients. I suggest storing bottled Negronis in the refrigerator and serving them on the rocks just the same. The ice won't melt as fast, but at least your Negroni will be nice and cold.

- 1 cup dry gin
- 1 cup Campari (see page 71)
- 8 ounces sweet vermouth

Using a funnel, pour the gin, Campari, and sweet vermouth directly into a clean 750-ml wine bottle. Seal with a cork or screw cap and gently rotate the bottle back and forth to mix. Chill in the freezer until cold.

For each serving, pour 2 ounces into a small chilled martini glass.

CARDINALE

{ Makes 12 cocktails }

- 1½ cups dry gin
- ¾ cup Campari (see page 71)
- 2 ounces dry vermouth

Using a funnel, pour the gin, Campari, and vermouth directly into a clean 750-ml bottle. Seal with a cork or screw cap and gently rotate the bottle back and forth to mix. Chill in the fridge until cold.

For each serving, fill a rocks glass with 3 or 4 ice cubes and top with 2 ounces of the cocktail.

After spending a day getting lost in Venice, it's worth pulling out a map to find Aciugheta, a wine bar and restaurant in Campo Santissimi Filippo e Giacomo not far from Piazza San Marco. Wind down with a glass of sparkling wine and a mini pizza topped with a little anchovy, or aciugheta.

ANCHOVY PIZZETTA
Aciugheta

⊹{ **Makes 6 to 8 aperitivo servings** }⊹

12 ounces Basic Focaccia Dough (page 100)

1 (14-ounce) can peeled San Marzano tomatoes, drained

Fine sea salt

Semolina, for dusting

6 ounces fresh fior di latte (cow's-milk) mozzarella, sliced

12 small oil-packed anchovies, rinsed

Divide the dough into quarters and then into 12 walnut-size pieces, about 1 ounce each.

Place the balls on an oiled baking sheet, cover with a kitchen towel, and let rise for another 15 to 30 minutes before baking. (If you don't plan to bake the pizzette immediately, cover and refrigerate the dough for up to 24 hours. Remove from the refrigerator 30 minutes before baking.)

To make the pizzette, place a pizza stone on the lowest shelf of an electric oven or directly on the floor of a gas oven. Preheat the oven to its maximum temperature, at least 450°F.

Put the tomatoes in a medium bowl. Pinch off and discard the harder tops with stems. Crush the tomatoes with a fork or separate into pieces by hand. Season lightly with salt.

On a floured work surface, flatten the balls of dough and stretch each of them to form a mini pizza, about 5 inches in diameter. Place 4 or 5 pizzette on a pizza peel dusted with semolina. Spread a spoonful of crushed tomatoes across each pizzetta and top with some of the mozzarella (½ ounce per pizzetta), torn into small pieces. Top each with an anchovy.

continued —»

Slide the pizzette onto the pizza stone and bake until the edges are dark brown or slightly charred, about 6 minutes.

Remove from the oven and let cool slightly on a rack. Serve immediately. Repeat with the remaining pizzette.

Notes If you plan to bake your pizzette before your guests arrive, reheat them on a baking sheet under a preheated broiler for a minute before serving.

Mastering the art of pizza making takes practice. There are many variables at play, including, but not limited to, the strength or protein content of the flour, the activeness of the yeast, the humidity and temperature of where the dough is left to rise, and the oven temperature. If you have a pizza dough recipe that works well for you, feel free to use it. Otherwise use this recipe as a starting point and start experimenting, adding a little extra water or flour if necessary or trying different brands and types of flour.

Octopus salad is served all along the Italian coast and varies according to the cook's preference. Gianni Bonaccorsi, chef-owner of Aciugheta, adds chopped tomatoes, when in season, to the standard combo of octopus, potatoes, and celery. Bonaccorsi insists that vinegar is the key to this recipe and what really awakens the flavor of the octopus. Frozen octopus works well here.

OCTOPUS SALAD WITH POTATOES AND CELERY *Aciugheta*

◊{ **Makes 6 to 8 aperitivo servings** }◊

1 medium octopus (about 2 pounds), cleaned

Handful of fresh herb stems (such as parsley, thyme, or oregano)

1 stalk celery plus 4 celery hearts, including leaves

3 waxy potatoes (about 1 pound)

3 vine-ripened tomatoes (about ¾ pound)

2 tablespoons chopped fresh flat-leaf parsley

¼ cup plus 2 tablespoons extra virgin olive oil

2 tablespoons red wine vinegar

2 teaspoons balsamic vinegar

1 clove garlic, finely chopped

1 teaspoon fine sea salt

Freshly ground black pepper

Put the octopus in a large pot and add enough water to cover. Add the stems of any herbs you have at home and a celery stalk cut in half. Bring to a boil over high heat. Reduce the heat to medium, cover, and let simmer until the octopus is tender. Cooking time may very dramatically from 30 minutes to more than an hour. (Test for tenderness by inserting a sharp knife into the thickest part of the octopus or by squeezing it directly with your hands.) When done, remove the pot from the heat and let the octopus cool in the cooking water.

Meanwhile, place the potatoes in a separate pot and add enough water to cover. Bring to a boil over high heat. Reduce the heat and simmer, partially covered, until the potatoes are tender,

continued —»

about 20 minutes. (If the tines of a fork can easily pierce the potatoes, they are done.) Drain, let the potatoes cool in the pot, then peel and dice them. Transfer the diced potatoes to a large bowl.

Drain and rinse the octopus. If the skin and tentacles slip off easily, remove them. If not, leave them on as they do at Aciugheta. Chop the octopus into bite-size pieces and add them to the potatoes. Chop the tomatoes, slice the celery hearts and chop the celery leaves, then add them to the bowl with the potatoes and octopus. Add the chopped parsley.

Prepare the dressing by whisking together the olive oil, both vinegars, the garlic, salt, and a couple grindings of pepper until emulsified. (Alternatively, you can add these ingredients to a jar, tighten the lid on the jar, and shake vigorously.) Drizzle the dressing over the salad and toss until well combined. Taste and adjust the salt if necessary.

Let the salad stand for at least an hour to allow the octopus to marinate in the dressing. Serve at room temperature in small bowls.

Note At Aciugheta, Bonaccorsi also serves a similar salad made with cuttlefish, celery, fennel, herbs, capers, and olive oil, and lemon zest and juice in place of the vinegar. Cuttlefish is more delicate than octopus and doesn't require the strong acidity. If you find cuttlefish at your local fish market, try preparing with this version at home.

SELECTED GUIDE

Carlo e Camilla in Segheria
Via Giuseppe Meda, 24
carloecamillainsegheria.it
open daily

Dry Cocktails & Pizza
Via Solferino, 33
02 63793414
drymilano.it
open daily

Giacomo Arengario
Via Guglielmo Marconi, 1
02 72093814
giacomoarengario.com
open daily

Giacomo Bistrot
Via Pasquale Sottocorno, 6
02 76022653
giacomobistrot.com
open daily

Fioraio Bianchi Caffè
Via Montebello, 7
02 29014390
fioraiobianchicaffe.it
closed Sunday

Il Luogo di Aimo e Nadia
Via Privata Raimondo
Montecuccoli, 6
aimoenadia.com
closed Sunday

Princi
Largo La Foppa, 2
02 6599013
princi.it
open daily

Ratanà
Via Gaetano de Castilla, 28
02 8712 8855
ratana.it
open daily

Rebelot del Pont
Ripa di Porta Ticinese, 55
02 84194720
rebelotdelpont.com
closed Tuesday

Rita & Cocktails
Via Angelo Fumagalli, 1
02 8372865
closed Monday

Taglio
Via Vigevano, 10
02 36534294
taglio.me
open daily

Un Posto a Milano
Via Privata Cuccagna, 2
02 5457785
unpostoamilano.it
closed Monday

Farther Afield
FLORENCE

Atrium Bar at Four Seasons Hotel Firenze
Borgo Pinti, 99
055 26261
fourseasons.com/florence
open daily

Caffè Giacosa (a.k.a. Cavalli Caffè)
Via della Spada, 10
055 2776328
cavallicaffè.com
open daily

Caffè Rivoire
Piazza della Signoria, 5
055 214412
rivoire.it
closed Monday

Faith Willinger's Tours
faithwillinger.com

Gucci Caffè
Piazza della Signoria, 10
055 75923827
guccimuseo.com
open daily

Procacci
for truffle butter sandwiches
Via de' Tornabuoni, 64r
055 211656
procacci1885.it
open daily

SE·STO on Arno
Piazza Ognissanti, 3
055 27151
sestoonarno.com
open daily

Chapter 3
PADUA

All'Ombra della Piazza
Via Pietro D'Abano, 16
049 8757343
closed Sunday

Al Sasso
Via Ronco, 11–Teolo (PD)
049 9925073
trattorialsasso.it
049 9925073
closed Wednesday

Box Caffè
Prato della Valle, 12
049 5916852
open daily

Galleria Corner
Piscopia, 19
049 8758595
boxcaffe.it
closed Sunday

Cafe Tinto
Via Vicenza, 20
049 8725713
diemmecaffe.com
closed Sunday

Enoteca Cortes
Riviera Paleocapa, 7
049 8719797
closed Monday

Enoteca Da Severino
Via del Santo, 44
049 650697
closed Sunday

Enoteca La Moscheta
Corso Milano, 58
049 660946
enotecalamoscheta.it
closed Sunday

Gran Caffè Diemme
Piazza dei Signori, 10
049 5913903
diemmecaffe.com
open daily

Folperia
for boiled baby octopus
Piazza della Frutta, 1

Il Calandrino
Via Liguria, 1–Sarmeola
di Rubano (PD)
049 630303
alajmo.it
open daily

Osteria L'Anfora
Via del Soncino, 13
049 656629
closed Sunday

Pelican Cafe
Corso Milano, 111
closed Monday

Farther Afield
ROME

Bar del Fico
Via della Pace 34/36
06 68891373
bardelfico.com
open daily

Barnum Cafe
Via del Pellegrino, 87
06 64760483
barnumcafe.com
open daily

Chiostro del Bramante
Via Arco della Pace, 5
06 68809035
chiostrodelbramante.it
open daily

Co.So
Via Braccio da Montone, 80
06 45435428
closed Sunday

Freni e Frazioni
Via del Politeama, 4/6
06 45497499
frenifrazioni.com
open daily

The Jerry Thomas Project
Vicolo Cellini, 30
06 96845937
thejerrythomasproject.it
open from 10 pm to 4 am
closed Sunday and Monday

Litro
Via Fratelli Bonnet, 5
06 45447639
vinerialitro.it
closed Sunday

Open Baladin
Via degli Specchi, 6
06 6838989
openbaladinroma.it
open daily

Stravinskij Bar at Hotel De Russie
Via del Babuino, 9
06 32888874
roccofortehotels.com
open daily

Chapter 4
VENICE

Aciugheta
Campo SS. Filippo e Giacomo / Castello 4357
041 5224292
open daily

All'Arco
Calle dell'Occhialer / San Polo 436
041 5205666
closed Sunday

Al Mercà
Campo Cesare Battisti / San Polo 213
closed Sunday

Al Portego
Calle Della Malvasia / Castello 6014
041 5229038
closed Sunday

Caffè Quadri
Piazza San Marco, 121
041 5222105
alajmo.it
open daily

Do Mori
Calle delle Do Spade / San Polo 429
041 5225401
closed Sunday

Estro
Calle Fianco de la Scuola / Dorsoduro 3778
041 4764914
estrovenezia.com
open daily

Gabbiano Bar at Belmond Hotel Cipriani
Giudecca 10
041 240801
belmond.com
open daily, spring to autumn

Harry's Bar
Calle Vallaresso / San Marco 1323
041 5285777
harrysbarvenezia.com
open daily

La Cantina
Campo San Felice / Cannaregio 3689
041 5228258
closed Sunday

Mascaretta
Calle Lunga Santa Maria Formosa
041 5230744
ostemaurolorenzon.it
open daily

Vino Vero
Fondamenta Misericorida / Cannaregio 2497
041 2750044
open daily

Wildner
Riva degli Schiavoni / Castello 4161
041 5227463
hotelwildner.com
closed Tuesday

SOURCES

A.G. Ferrari
agferrari.com
San Francisco–based Italian source for specialty pantry items.

Astor Wine & Spirits
astorwines.com
Shop for imported Italian aperitivo liqueurs like Campari and other Campari-like red aperitivo bitters produced by Cappelletti, Luxardo, and Meletti.

Bar Products
barproducts.com
Online source for shakers, bar spoons, and glassware.

BevMo!
bevmo.com
With locations across the United States, BevMo! is a go-to source for aperitivo cocktail basics: Campari, sweet vermouth, and amari like Cynar.

Buon Italia
buonitalia.com
Sells imported Italian goods including stracchino cheese for preparing Ligurian Cheese Focaccia (see pages 60–61).

Cask Store
caskstore.com
San Francisco–based source for wine-based aperitifs, cocktail bitters, and top-notch soda waters, plus much more.

Cocktail Kingdom
cocktailkingdom.com
Alternative source for bar products such as ice trays, bitters, and syrups.

Di Palo's
dipaloselects.com
Source for almost every Italian food export. Open since 1925 in New York City's Little Italy.

Eataly
eataly.com
With stores currently located in New York City and Chicago, this Italian food wonderland stocks its shelves with everything from pantry staples like extra virgin olive oils and traditional balsamic vinegars to specialty items, such as cedrata (see pages 32 and 43), chinotto (see page 57), and a wide array of Italian craft beers.

Formaggio Kitchen
formaggiokitchen.com
Online source for a wide selection of imported Italian artisanal cheeses, as well as other gourmet foods.

Fra' Mani
framani.com
Chef Paul Bertolli produces great Italian-style salumi available online and at specialty grocers.

Gustiamo
gustiamo.com
Online retailer and wholesaler of well-sourced imported Italian products ranging from saffron threads to tomatoes.

Kalustyan's
kalustyans.com
Manhattan-based Indian food market selling all kinds of herbs, spices, and specialty flours such as chickpea and spelt.

King Arthur Flour
kingarthurflour.com
Great source for flour and yeast for preparing aperitivo staples such as focaccia, grissini, and pizzette.

La Quercia
laquercia.us
Iowa-based producer of Italian-style cured pork products like prosciutto crudo and guanciale.

Murray's Cheese Shop
murrayscheese.com
Extensive selection of imported Italian artisanal cheeses.

Sur La Table
surlatable.com
Reliable nationwide source for top-quality cookware and kitchen tools.

Williams-Sonoma
williams-sonoma.com
Nationwide source for professional cooking equipment and gourmet pantry items like extra virgin olive oil and flaky sea salt.

Zingerman's
zingermans.com
Based in Ann Arbor, Michigan, Zingerman's is an excellent source for harder-to-find, quality ingredients such as salt-packed anchovies, caperberries, and cured meats.

CONVERSION CHART

All conversions are approximate.

LIQUID CONVERSIONS		WEIGHT CONVERSIONS		OVEN TEMPERATURES		
U.S.	Metric	U.S. U.K.	Metric	°F	Gas Mark	°C
1 tsp	5 ml	½ oz	14 g	250	½	120
1 tbs	15 ml	1 oz	28 g	275	1	140
2 tbs	30 ml	1½ oz	43 g	300	2	150
3 tbs	45 ml	2 oz	57 g	325	3	165
¼ cup	60 ml	2½ oz	71 g	350	4	180
⅓ cup	75 ml	3 oz	85 g	375	5	190
⅓ cup + 1 tbs	90 ml	3½ oz	100 g	400	6	200
⅓ cup + 2 tbs	100 ml	4 oz	113 g	425	7	220
½ cup	120 ml	5 oz	142 g	450	8	230
⅔ cup	150 ml	6 oz	170 g	475	9	240
¾ cup	180 ml	7 oz	200 g	500	10	260
¾ cup + 2 tbs	200 ml	8 oz	227 g	550	Broil	290
1 cup	240 ml	9 oz	255 g			
1 cup + 2 tbs	275 ml	10 oz	284 g			
1¼ cups	300 ml	11 oz	312 g			
1⅓ cups	325 ml	12 oz	340 g			
1½ cups	350 ml	13 oz	368 g			
1⅔ cups	375 ml	14 oz	400 g			
1¾ cups	400 ml	15 oz	425 g			
1¾ cups + 2 tbs	450 ml	1 lb	454 g			
2 cups (1 pint)	475 ml					
2½ cups	600 ml					
3 cups	720 ml					
4 cups (1 quart)	945 ml (1,000 ml is 1 liter)					

INDEX